Mario Andretti

The Man Who Can Win Any Kind of Race

Mario Andretti

The Man Who Can Win
Any Kind of Race

**Produced by Lyle Kenyon Engel
and the editorial staff of *Auto Racing* magazine**

ARCO PUBLISHING COMPANY, INC.
New York

Editorial Staff

Jeff Scott
George Engel
Marla Ray

Photography

Arnie de Brier
Kenneth H. Coles
Daytona International Speedway
Edward Deaux
George Engel
Lyle K. Engel
Joe Farkas
Ford Motor Company
Harry Goode
Jim Hahn
Indianapolis Motor Speedway

Bud Jones
Nick Longworth
John P. May
John R. Mahoney
David Phipps
Photo Graphics
John Plow
Gerald Schmitt
Jeff Scott
Barry M. Tenin
Dennis Torres

Published by ARCO PUBLISHING COMPANY, INC.
219 Park Avenue South, New York, N.Y. 10003
Copyright © Lyle Kenyon Engel, 1970
All Rights Reserved
Library of Congress Catalog Number 79-103076
ISBN 0-668-02193-4
Printed in the United States of America

Contents

Introduction

A lot of good things have happened to me in more than twenty years of automobile racing. And among the best of the good things has been my racing and personal relationship with a fearless, graceful little athlete named Mario Andretti.

When Mario first came to Indianapolis Motor Speedway—and even before that—I felt a kind of kinship with him—not because we are both Italian— we are both racers in the best sense of the word. Like me, Mario had battled his way up from the very bottom of the heap. That takes guts and guts are the No. 1 essential in auto racing, whether you are battling a bucking, spinning race car at 160 miles an hour, fighting the establishment for what you believe is right or just trying to get started in one of the world's truly tough professions.

I had heard about Mario before he came to Indianapolis. When you are Andy Granatelli, you hear about promising youngsters all the time. And when I sought him out to chat that first year and the years immediately afterward, I found him modest, considerate of others and at the same time totally aggressive underneath it all. I knew, back when he was named Rookie of the Year after a brilliant first-time performance at Indy, that someday he would drive for me—just as I have always known that one of my cars would someday win the "500." It was just a question of how and when.

When we made the deal with Mario early in 1969 whereby he became part of the STP Racing Team, I was quietly happy. People around me tell me that all of a sudden I got easier to live with. I guess my great confidence in Mario was the reason. Mario's early win for us at Hanford in April of 1969 gave truth to that feeling. Despite the roadblocks in the path to an Indy victory, I never really doubted that Mario would do it for us. And of course he did, and the Impossible Dream came true for all of us.

So, I commend to you the life story of Mario Andretti. He has a lot to tell everyone and I know you will enjoy getting to know this brave, skilled, classy little racing driver as I know him. He's all here, in the pages of this book.

Anthony (Andy) Granatelli
Director, STP Racing Team

The Highest Goal Is Finally Reached

The time was 2:10 P.M. The date, May 30, 1969. On the back straight of the world-famous Indianapolis Motor Speedway a bright red racing car was completing its final lap. In less than thirty seconds a young Italian-American would, for the first time in his brilliant career, take the checkered flag from Pat Vidan. Vidan sensed the drama of this impending moment, but he remained calm as always, having flagged home many winners of this classic event.

But the thousands of fans packing the huge stands on the fourth turn and main straightaway were buzzing with the stimulating excitement of seeing one of their favorite drivers finally make the rewarding trip to Victory Lane. As Mario Andretti moved into the final turn, the conversational buzzing quickly changed to roaring cheers.

In the pit area, virtually all the racing car crews and chief mechanics were standing, looking as one man to the finish line. But there was *one* exception. Sitting, as though frozen, in his canvas beach chair was a chubby, Buddha-like man staring almost blankly across the track. The men around him were pounding each other on the back and shouting themselves hoarse with joy. But Andy Granatelli seemed unmoved by the wild scene and the sound of the roaring crowds which engulfed him.

Spectators near the Granatelli pit were naturally puzzled by this seeming indifference. After all, the bright No. 2 car was his, plastered with giant STP decals.

A rare moment for Andy and Mario—peace and quiet at the Indianapolis Motor Speedway as they plan for the future. ▶

The hard-sought goal is finally reached. Mario and Andy
have found their way to Indy's Victory Lane.

But the mystified fans had, perhaps, forgotten that Granatelli had twice before been within minutes of victory, then fate had ruled otherwise.

In 1967 the most advanced racing car in Indianapolis history, after total domination of the other 32 cars in the field, had snapped a six-dollar bearing three laps from what had seemed to be a smashing victory. The STP Turbocar rolled into the pits with driver Parnelli Jones frozen with shock and disbelief.

Then in 1968, with its effectiveness muted by the United States Auto Club, another STP Turbocar took command of the "500," this time joined by two sister cars. Here the predicted domination did not materialize. After eight laps a determined Bobby Unser had gone by Joe Leonard, who had set a record when taking the qualifying pole position.

However, as the race neared its climax, Leonard was out in front once more. Then the stage was set for another cruel twist of racing misfortune.

About fifteen laps from the finish a crash brought out the yellow flag. By racing law Unser was forced to hold his position. The fans roared their disapproval, for it would have been an anticlimax to end this exciting race under a yellow flag.

Suddenly, with about ten laps remaining, the green was out again and Leonard mashed his accelerator for a burst of power which would carry him easily the rest of the way. But with equal suddenness, there was no power. The silent screamer coasted to a stop at the first turn. It was dead. And once more Granatelli's twenty-two-year dream of winning this great classic was destroyed, as was a small fuel pump shaft in not only Leonard's car, but Pollard's as well. The third Turbocar, driven by Graham Hill, had lost a wheel and crashed earlier in the race. Again Granatelli's dream of victory was wiped out.

Now in 1969 as Mario came through the fourth turn, Andy's mind was full of the bitter memories of the past two years. It could happen again. But as his car flashed safely across the finish line, its screaming turbo Ford engine almost drowned out by the engulfing roar of the fans, the portly Granatelli bounded out of his chair as if propelled by a cannon.

He began running down the long pit straight toward Victory Lane, his brothers Vince and Joe trailing. Then he burst into the already jammed enclosure, just as an equally ecstatic Andretti rolled his oil-smudged STP Oil Treatment Special in off the track.

In front of all the world, the burly, emotional Granatelli planted a wet kiss on the grease-smudged face of his hero.

And that was the moment of glory for both men. Mario had waited four years for his pinnacle of triumph, Andy Granatelli, twenty-three years.

For both the 1969 "500" was "Italianapolis."

The Beginning

Mario Andretti's spectacular climb to racing glory was quick, but it was not a simple, rose-covered ascent.

This young champion-to-be was born in Trieste, Italy on February 28, 1940. That was the year when Indianapolis immortal Wilbur Shaw won his second straight "500." It might have been a good omen for Mario that Shaw won that race in an Italian Grand Prix Maserati, which had been revamped to turn left at the giant Brickyard.

Mrs. Andretti also gave birth that night to Aldo, Mario's identical twin. Aldo's hopes for emulating his now famous brother would be sadly frustrated. But that comes later in our story.

Young boys in Italy accord racing drivers the same kind of hero worship that American youth pay to baseball and football players. Mario's idol was the magnificent Italian ace, Ferrari Grand Prix driver, Alberto Ascari. Today, in his sumptuous home in suburban Nazareth, Pennsylvania, Mario has an oil painting of Ascari letting it all hang out in a GP Ferrari.

As the Andretti family was not well to do, Mario and Aldo were forced to pool their limited funds in order to see as much racing as possible.

One race in particular stands out in Mario's memory. He was fourteen at the time: "The 1954 Monza Grand Prix was the race that jelled a decision for me. Ascari and the great Juan Manuel Fangio fought a classic wheel to wheel duel. It was the most exciting big car race I'd ever seen.

"Before that race I hoped I might some day be a racing driver. After that race I *had* to be a driver."

About the time Mario and Aldo were dreaming of some day when they might be able to afford a racing car of some kind, *any* kind, the Italian government chose to virtually underwrite a program for developing a new breed of Italian drivers.

His early racing career in the United States was at the wheel of modified stock cars like this one that he drove at Nazareth (Pennsylvania) Speedway in 1959.

A wealthy racing enthusiast, Count Giovanni Lurani, created a new class of open wheel racing cars, which was dubbed Formula Junior. The chassis were slightly smaller versions of the big Grand Prix Formula 1 cars, fitted with much smaller engines.

The special class would serve as a racing laboratory for searching out budding talent, as Ferrari and Maserati were worried about the shrinking pool of Italian drivers.

"Aldo and I located a sponsor for a $300 car [Yes, racing cars were much cheaper then!] for Formula Junior racing," Mario recalls. "It was a Stanguellini chassis powered by an 85-horsepower Fiat engine. Aldo and I swapped off driving and crewing for each other on alternate weekends. We had a ball."

It must be noted here that in Europe and in Mexico a young aspiring driver

With pit crew in his Mataka-owned midget in which he won three races in one day.

did not have to be twenty-one, as required in most major racing clubs in the United States. For example, Pedro Rodriguez began racing when he was fifteen. The late Jimmy Clark began at seventeen in Scotland.

"We built up a loyal following among local fans," says Mario, "and we did pretty well."

As the Andretti family was far from wealthy, the father decided that America would hold a better future. The Andrettis had relatives living in Nazareth, Pennsylvania. They served as sponsors, as immigration laws require that before a foreign family can emigrate to the United States, there must be assurance they will have a place to live and a future. This, of course, is simply to ensure some kind of financial security.

After the Andrettis arrived in Nazareth, it wasn't long before the mechanically oriented Mario got a job in a local gas station. Both Mario and Aldo had worked on race cars in Italy, eagerly soaking up all the lore they could, so Mario's natural bent toward the mechanical thing paid off.

Says Mario: "This job supplied me with a lot of personal contacts with regard to the local racing scene. Also, I was able to learn English a lot faster." Today Mario speaks English with practically no accent.

Racing was strong in Pennsylvania. There were a host of dirt tracks and there were many eager drivers—men like Red Riegel and Jud Larson. Naturally, Mario and Aldo quickly got involved in the action.

It might be mentioned here that Papa Andretti was not overjoyed about his sons' getting hooked on racing. Of course, his attitude was not helped by Mario's accident while cranking it on a back road near Nazareth in 1957. He was tossed out of the street machine after whacking a tree. Mario sustained a broken nose, which is about the most serious injury he's ever had, even during his racing career.

The Andrettis' first major racing venture was initiated in a 1948 Hudson Hornet. They converted it into a sportsman and began to run the Pennsylvania dirt track circuit in 1959.

Mario warms up to this recollection: "That was no junker. A lot of thought and hard work went into it. A friend had stockpiled a lot of good dope about Marshall Teague's equipment. We learned about spring rates and shock absorber positioning. Whatever we needed, we had it."

For our younger readers, in the middle 1950s the Hudson Hornet was the king of the oval tracks, and Marshall Teague was the Richard Petty of that era of stock car racing.

This racing would serve as the base for Mario's skills in setting up his Championship cars. Today's Indy car, with its delicate, complex suspension, can pick up or lose critical seconds a lap, depending upon the suspension settings. Therefore, it's vital for a driver to be able to translate to his crew what settings are right for his style of driving.

As Mario says: "After running awhile, you get to know what you want and

◄ In his T.Q. midget at the Teaneck (New Jersey) Armory in 1959.

you set up the equipment where it feels best. A lot of drivers go like hell when the car's right. But if the car isn't right, they can't help themselves. It's not necessarily a talent you are *born* with. It's a talent you *acquire*.

"I always want to be there when my car is being set up, especially if we are running on a new track. Then the crew and I put our heads together and try new things, as I want to know what's going on. This way you know what to correct if it's called for.

"There are some big time drivers with whom I race today, who simply pull in after a couple of practice laps and say, 'This thing runs like a pig.' Well, the poor mechanic has to guess what the trouble is. You've got to *know* what's happening with a racing car, whether it's porpoising or doing this or that on the turns. Then your crew can get things working properly. It's really no more than telling a doctor where the pain is before he examines you."

Meanwhile the Andretti boys were beginning to carve out a name on the local tracks. Mario especially appreciated the way Jud Larson and Red Riegel helped to show him the shortest way around a track.

"Some guys want to stick you in the wall to teach you," Mario says, "Jud Larson had another approach. I was barreling along in front in a race one day and all of a sudden, I felt myself losing my car. I looked back and Jud had his nose right on my tail. He was nudging me around letting me know he had me under control.

"That was only *one* time. He taught me other things, too. Guys like Jud and Red break you easy, if they can. They show a kid the tricks of our trade. They show you how not to do things that could hurt other people if you're young and reckless."

Mario and Aldo tried not to be harebrained on the track, but they were hard drivers, in there every minute. In the fall of 1958 at Hatfield, Pennsylvania, it was Aldo's turn at the wheel. Suddenly the car went out of control, smashing against a fence. Aldo was rushed to the hospital with a brain concussion.

At this stage of the boys' racing career, Papa Andretti still had a strong aversion to such "foolishness." After Aldo had been checked into the hospital, Mario came up with a fanciful piece of information that Aldo had fallen off the cab of a pickup truck while watching a race. Whether the "story" really was accepted, we're not quite sure.

There is a sad footnote to Aldo's accident. When he got back into a racing car, he was not as skilled, it seemed, as he had been. When Mario's career began to climb in USAC, Aldo was grimly determined to do as well. But it was not destined to happen.

Aldo tried his hand at midgets and sprint cars, but with little success. He thirsted for the USAC Championship Trail, but USAC said no. Finally, during the 1969 season, while running a sprint car event, Aldo crashed badly, sustaining serious head injuries. He recovered, but it's pretty much a sure thing that he won't race again. Aldo and his wife now live in Indianapolis. He often appears at various Championship races when Mario is running and reporters never fail to confuse the two. For Mario and Aldo are as alike as two peas in a pod.

Mario began to establish himself as a driver. He had that key factor vitally important to anyone seeking success in his chosen field—determination. It was not merely a case of wanting to win this or that race, Mario *had* to win. Now he was driving everything: jalopies, three-quarter midgets, sprints and standard size midgets. If it was something on wheels that would go, Mario would run it.

"I've always wanted to be an all-around driver, to be able to handle any car on any surface," says Mario.

Open wheel, pure racing cars had always been Mario's primary aim. He also wanted to get into road racing, but this is virtually impossible without a sponsor. Amateur road racing has always been a rich man's sport. He would, however, later score in an extraordinary fashion driving sports cars for Ferrari and Ford.

When he reached the legal racing age of twenty-one, Mario got his first ride. To quote him: "It was a real 'box.' I ran at West Lebanon, New York. I managed to finish fourth and made the feature. I really had trouble sorting it out. I just didn't know which way it was going to go."

Eventually Mario worked his way up to the top rank of sprint car drivers. In 1964 he had run twenty races, finished eleven times in the first five and won once. He was third behind champion Don Branson and second-placed Jud Larson in the national standings.

Mario gives full credit, however, to the basic proving grounds of midget competition. He says this provided him with a solid base in preparing for his eventual brilliant career in Championship cars.

As he points out: "Although sprint cars were very helpful, the real training ground for me was the midget racing I did with ARDC. One of the negative factors in my early sprint car racing was that I couldn't get a good ride.

"Later I managed to find a really competitive midget, an Offy. Before get-

A painting of World Champion Alberto Ascari, the man who crystallized Mario's desire to race, hangs on the wall of his den.

ting into this machine, I had just been running around the track, not getting anywhere. Now I began winning. It was a whole new ball game. It gave me a shot of confidence. Previously, I had been driving a box, and I began asking myself was it me or the car that was bad. When I started in those early sprint car days, to me anything that had four wheels, a racing car look and a steering wheel was a real racing car.

"I was satisfied with just being able to sit in such a car. I never really gave a thought as to how the car actually worked. Finally, when I got into a real piece of machinery, wow! The guys who used to whiz by me, those you wouldn't see until after the race, were now the same guys I was running in contention with. It changed my whole attitude. Things really began working for me.

"I did some of my best racing in midgets. I used to run a lot of them. Sometimes I'd run as many as five races in one day.

"Once, in 1963, I won three races in one day. I won at the Flemington Fairgrounds in New Jersey. That evening I rushed over to Hatfield, Pennsylvania. There was a feature to be run which had previously been rained out. I won the heat and the regular feature after that. Those were the races which really developed my racing technique."

The break that all budding champions hope and pray for finally happened to Mario Andretti in 1964, when Clint Brawner came to see him race.

"I had been running the USAC circuits by this time," recalls Mario, "and I was at Terre Haute, Indiana. Clint Brawner's regular driver, Chuck Hulse, had been hurt. Clint asked me if I'd like to come over to his place and look at his equipment. I played it cool, saying I might be over there tomorrow. Actually I was there at five the next morning, waiting for the place to open."

Oddly enough Mario's big moment did not come at once. As he tells it:

"The race was to be at Langhorne for Championship cars. Clint didn't like the track. I can understand his thinking. Langhorne was a tough place to run, as it was still dirt then.

"He advised that I skip it and then we could get together for the next one. I said to heck with *that*. Then I got in touch with Tommy Hinnershitz [another former top midget champion]. He was the mechanic on Lee Glessner's car. So we ran Langhorne with it.

"We kinda pulled a surprise. We out-qualified Brawner's car and finished ahead of it. I have to admit I was a bit up tight about Langhorne. It was quite dangerous, especially for a rookie driver."

Clint Brawner and Mario finally did get together and a deal was made to drive the Al Dean cars.

This would be the turning point for Mario Andretti. From here he was headed for bigger and better things.

The Man Who Put Mario On the Road to Glory

No matter how talented a driver may be, he can only extract so much from his car. Therefore a must for a champion driver is a first class chief mechanic.

Mario Andretti was doubly fortunate in having master mechanic Clint Brawner. Not only did Brawner bring Andretti into three national titles and the highest of all goals for a USAC driver, the "500," but he also brought Mario into major league racing.

This weather-beaten crew chief from Phoenix, Arizona has a record that few of his wrench-twisting associates can equal. During eighteen years of preparing racing cars, Brawner has won over fifty Championship races. He has groomed two drivers to six National Championships. Out of a possible 268 National Championship races, he has entered cars in 255, qualified 235 times and his cars have started 232 times.

His drivers were top notch. With Jimmy Bryan, the legendary, cigar chewing three-time National Champion, Brawner won seventeen Championship races. Not officially counted was the blazing victory by Bryan at the international 500-miler at Monza, Italy in 1957, in a Dean Van Lines Special.

The late Eddie Sachs was also a Dean Van Lines driver. He was a three-time Championship race winner in a Brawner-prepared car.

Clint reached his all-time high of checkered flags with Mario Andretti: thirty, including the elusive goal of all drivers and mechanics, the Indy "500."

Brawner's record is truly astonishing. He won six National Championships

Checking his car's springs, Andretti demonstrates one of the reasons Clint Brawner likes him so much. His mechanical knowledge and willingness ▶ to work in addition to his ability as a driver make him an asset to any team.

—"I passed A. J. this year," says Clint with a big grin—1954-56-57, 1965-66-69.

At Indianapolis, Brawner has had not only his victory in 1969 but also two second place finishes and three thirds. His cars have had the pole four times.

It was Dean Van Lines, owned by the late Al Dean, that launched Mario Andretti on his meteoric career. But it was the cagey, race-wise Clint Brawner who decided that the young Italian-American had that certain quality of which championship drivers are made.

"It was Terre Haute, where I had first seen him," recalls Brawner. "I went over to watch him work and perform. I watched Mario working on his car, making his own tire selection and setting up the chassis.

"He was really hard working and ambitious and knowing a little about racing, I knew right away that he was clued in about what he was doing. I'd heard about Mario some three years before from Chris Economaki and a fellow in Foyt's pit crew. I was really impressed."

Brawner also points out that there are many top notch drivers who are great on a race track as long as the car is set up right. But when something goes wrong in handling, or some other involved problem, they just can't explain what's wrong to the crew. They are not tuned in to the mechanical end. With today's complicated cars, especially the suspension, a driver must be able to quickly analyze the problem in handling and be able to translate this to his crew.

"After watching Mario that afternoon," says Brawner, "I told my wife that I was tired of going with these old guys that have been around a long time and I thought I'd try another new kid and spend about a year with him. It turned out to be a good choice."

That was the understatement of the year. It turned out that the Brawner-Andretti alliance would last five years, resulting in Brawner's first Indy "500" win, plus three National Championships.

When pressed for comparisons between legendary heroes such as Jimmy Bryan and A. J. Foyt, this is Clint's candid evaluation:

"I think Mario is a far better race driver now than Jimmy Bryan, if you put them together on a track today. However, you might say Bryan was king of the dirt. He was the best I ever saw. But you must realize there were far more dirt races in USAC during Jimmy's time. Mario is great on dirt tracks. He's proved that by winning the Hoosier Hundred twice, plus his other wins. But today most of the key races are being run on paved tracks.

"Now take Foyt. I think Foyt's probably the world's greatest race driver. With all his money and his greatness, he'll still get out there and run. He proved it at Milwaukee [1969] when he unloaded that dirt car and went right out there and drove the hell out of it."

A. J. had blown the engine in his Coyote Ford. So he went and ran the

A familiar sight at tracks across the country, Andretti suited up and ready to race and Brawner hiding his sun-sensitive neck under a bright bandana.

He quickly adapted to the modern, lightweight, rear-engined racer,
and was startlingly competitive in his Indianapolis debut.

event in his dirt track machine. Even though much outclassed, he came in ninth! Then at the Trenton 300, Foyt blew an engine in practice, so he borrowed one of Mario's engines.

This really impressed Brawner: "Foyt went right out there with our engine and beat our time. This is great, you know.

"Now Mario, I'd say, is the second greatest. He runs the banks [stock car superspeedways]. Mario will run anything on wheels. He runs just as hard for a small purse as a big one. I would say that Mario has come a long way in the short time he's been running."

During the early years of his Championship competition, Mario now and then would push a little too hard at a track to grab the pole position. He would put the car into the wall. Brawner revealed a problem he had encountered that first year which was also a handicap to Mario which few know about today.

"We found out later in the year we had a chassis problem which we corrected," Clint recalls. "That's why we came back and looked so great in the next two years. Mario had not had the experience as a driver and I lacked experience with coil spring suspension. It was about November when I found it out. You see, my car is based on a Brabham design. So one day Jimmy McElreath drove our car and then a Lotus. After he came back in Jimmy said, comparing the two, the Lotus drove like a Cadillac. Right then I figured we have got to be bottoming out and bouncing on something solid. So I went home and said to Mario, 'We've got the wrong springs.' So we changed them. From then on, it was a whole new race car."

Shifting back to the early days with Mario, Clint points out that Andretti was a good listener. He took advice: "He knew I had the years of experience on a lot of things in racing. He paid attention."

Then Clint looks at Mario today.

"He could become the all-time point champion because I see Foyt retiring in the next couple of years. I wish A. J. would. There's really nothing more for him to win, except a fourth Indy Five Hundred."

Clint seems to warm up when talking about the team itself: "Our team was good for each other. Jim McGee is going to be one of the greatest mechanics as he gets older. Times are much better now than they were when I started. I've tried to train Jim and help guide him in the way I do things. We have had a really good operation."

Brawner's answer to whether it's tougher today to run a racing car than it was ten or fifteen years ago: "It certainly is, three times the work it used to be. You know, I can't understand how some of these small crews of three or four will get together two cars and bring them to a track. We've got about six people preparing one car and we have to work day and night sometimes. For example, take this particular race at Trenton. We got here about two this morning and rolled it in and finally got it set up by five. Gee, I've reached a point where I'm going to have to start training someone else, I guess. I'll be missing some of these races one day and I'll have to worry about someone packing for me. I've made up a check list, something like a pilot's check sheet. It has such odds and ends as my straw hat and Andy's chair. If I don't, somebody's sure to forget them."

Clint tells how he feels about dirt track racing today, with the increased schedule. The fact that it calls for an entirely different car to be cared for and fed—that is, a dirt track machine.

"Well, outside of the Hoosier Hundred, which is a classic and quite lucrative, I think we ought to drop the dirt tracks and leave them to the sprint car boys. But whenever I've been under the pressure of being in the top two or three positions in the standings—and that's been the case with most of my racing career—I've made the dirt track races. As you know, I've missed very few races during my entire career. You've really got to keep in good physical shape for a routine like this. You can't be sick or take time off or go lolly-gagging around. I'll tell you, I *have* felt real bad at times, but I had to keep pushing, for I had a goal to make. So now that I'm getting older [fifty-two], it's a real rough thing keeping up with these kids."

Looking at Clint Brawner today, he seems to be able to keep up with anyone.

His trademark at any track is a combination of wide-brimmed straw hat and a train engineer's neckerchief. This comes from inheriting a sun allergy, which can give him real trouble if his face and neck are not protected.

Brawner's depth of know-how reaches back to 1931. He worked in a machine shop where many racing car parts were turned out. He began to build midgets. This was his steady diet until 1950. He had always wanted to build a Championship car after endless pilgrimages to the Brickyard. This he finally accomplished in 1951. The car was driven by Bobby Ball and finished fifth.

In 1952 he became chief mechanic. The next year Clint began what would be a fourteen-year association with the late Al Dean for the Dean Van Lines Specials.

When this true sportsman died in 1967—Dean never sought a profit from racing—Mario Andretti, who had now come into his own both professionally and financially, bought out the team.

Starting in 1969 the unit was operated under the STP banner.

It's sad that Brawner will not be back with Mario. They have decided to go their separate ways. Clint will now prepare cars for Roger McCluskey who has severed his Championship ties with A. J. Foyt.

Mario learned much from Clint Brawner and, in turn, Mario brought his "discoverer" the greatest number of victories in his long career.

Mario Comes Into His Own

The late Al Dean was a kindly, quiet man who loved racing. He sponsored cars because he loved the sport, not seeking a livelihood from it. Dean enjoyed a comfortable income from his sizable moving van business, so he had no axe to grind. The sport, and especially the United States Auto Club, benefited from his deep interest in racing.

Dean helped the careers of many drivers, including the late Jimmy Bryan. Bryan was typical of the no-holds-barred driver of an almost bygone era. He was tough, brutally strong. He was ideally suited to the big, tank-like racing cars that were the roadsters.

Also a Dean driver was Bob Sweikert. He eventually became a National Champion in 1955. Then in 1958 Dean signed a promising young rookie by the name of A. J. Foyt. In 1959 it was again Foyt, who was then setting his gradual pace which would lead him to five National Championships. In 1961 the late Eddie Sachs drove for Dean Van Lines, the best break of his storm-tossed career. Dean also had Troy Ruttman.

Mario was fortunate in that he was able to join a racing team with plenty of depth and can't-be-bought racing lore. It was not a low budget operation. Dean went first class all the way, plus having a brilliant chief mechanic in the form of Clint Brawner.

When he first tried the front-engined Offy Championship car, Mario encountered a few initial stages of overeagerness in trying to sort it out.

Jim McGee, then a young member of the Brawner team, recalls that Mario, with his go-go attitude, spun the car in his first race before the warmup laps were completed. But McGee, along with the whole crew, quickly grew to respect Mario from the beginning of their relationship, as he combined techni-

cal know-how with that burning ambition to win that has got to be a basic quality in every would-be champion.

McGee makes this note: "One thing we learned to admire about Mario is his stamina. As for his mental outlook toward racing, well, he is one in a million. A driver must be able to concentrate, but he can't get hypnotized. The amazing thing about Mario is that he never moves back. He never loses his speed or position in a race, unless there is something failing in his car."

When Mario made his debut on the Championship Trail, the fans were both amused and captivated. This pint-sized young man was a far cry from the muscular types such as the 200-pound Bill Cheesbourg and the powerfully built A. J. Foyt. It's said that when Andretti first appeared on a USAC big car championship lineup card, Foyt asked, "Mario who?" He would discover some startling answers in 1965.

Then there was a sarcastic newsman, who amused himself by printing silly, snide remarks about Andretti's size. Mario shot back a fast answer: "I'm here to drive this car, not wrestle it."

Mario had also another minor handicap. He entered big car racing with a distorted reputation for being a fencebuster and a hairy driver. The most accurate peg to hang on Andretti is that he's an all-out charger. So are Foyt, Bobby and Al Unser and Dan Gurney. That's the name of the game.

"Sure, I'm eager," Mario agrees, "and so is every other major driver in a race. We're all out to win."

Andretti was behind the wheel of the Dean Van Lines Special No. 7 for the last eight races of the 1964 season. He managed a third place finish in the Milwaukee 200, accumulating enough points to end up eleventh in the Championship car standings.

The following year would show the promise of things to come. At the end of the 1964 season Clint Brawner quickly realized that the front-engined road-sters had reached the end of the line. Even though Clint might be termed a veteran of the old roadster school, and had enjoyed many victories with these big monsters, he was shrewd enough to see the handwriting on the wall. In 1963 and 1964 Jimmy Clark had shown clearly that the then new rear-engined Lotus concept was the car of the future.

Over the winter months, Brawner and Jim McGee fashioned their own lightweight Indy car, but elected to use a time proven Offy in the rear, instead of the Ford twin-cam engine favored by A. J. Foyt, Jim Clark and Parnelli Jones.

If one were to single out a race that stamped Mario's budding talents firmly in the fans' minds, it had to be the USAC big car season-opener at Phoenix, Arizona. Phoenix is not an easy track, but Andretti showed quickly that he could find the shortest way around. Actually his car was not a new lightweight Lotus concept, but an altered roadster. So it was a case of his trying to stack up against lighter and faster cars.

◀ Much impressed with the performance of Brabham's car at Indy, Brawner custom-tailored this Brabham-based car around Andretti and a Ford engine.

Shown here hounding A. J. Foyt during the 1965 Hoosier Grand Prix, Mario captured his first Championship win in this inaugural USAC road course race.

During practice runs, Mario ran his new car up to 120 mph for a short-lived world record for a mile track—something which he would do many times later in his career. When official qualifying was over, Mario was third fastest with a 117.188 mph.

There he was, a rookie, sitting in two rows full of hot Ford-powered Lotus-type machinery. The fans were now talking up this new arrival. But many of the more seasoned onlookers took a skeptical "let's wait and see" attitude. After all, many a hot shot, like a Fourth of July rocket, burned brightly but briefly, then fizzled into oblivion.

When the green flag was dropped, the Lotus Fords quickly snatched the lead, which surprised no one. As the race progressed, it seemed it would be a case of which Lotus would dominate.

With his major USAC competitor A. J. Foyt, who no longer asks, "Mario Who?"

Suddenly the fans were stimulated by the sight of this fellow, Mario "Ondrotti"—it would be awhile before track announcers would properly pronounce his name—beginning to press the Ford-powered lightweights.

On the 46th lap A. J. Foyt was slightly jolted when Mario "Who" steamed by him, passing another Indy craftsman, Rodger Ward, at the same time. There he was, in his first major Championship race, out in front.

Now even the most skeptical of fans were jumping up and down. They were seeing a real race!

The young man from Nazareth stayed out in front until the 110th lap. Then the bubble of victory burst. Says Mario:

"I was watching Johnny Rutherford and setting up to lap him when his car went out of control. I had to spin into the infield to avoid a collision."

Mario got back into the race, after having been penalized for a push start, and resumed his electrifying road show. Going flat out Andretti began lapping cars left and right, but he was just too far down behind the leaders to make up that lost time. However, he did complete 148 laps and wound up in sixth place.

But the fans went home talking about this young man from Pennsylvania. Many correctly predicted big things for him.

Next was the Trenton big car race. In this 100-miler, which is the curtain raiser for the Indy "500," Mario qualified fifth and finished second. He was on his way.

Now it was time to get ready for Indianapolis.

Even though Al Dean was very much attached to the classic Offenhauser roadster, he was not one to stand in the way of racing progress and the obviously brilliant potential of Mario. Therefore it was decided that, in order to be competitive in the "500," they would drop the roadster. Brawner and McGee had been at work on a totally new car, based on a design by Australian Jack Brabham. It would be Ford powered.

Brawner had been much impressed with Brabham when he ran the very first modern rear-engined car at Indianapolis in 1961. Later Jack had produced his own cars. It was clear that the quiet man from "down under" knew what he was doing, so Brawner chose to base his car on Brabham's design. The cockpit was custom tailored to Mario. He was five feet six and weighed in at 134. Though small in stature, Mario is exceptionally strong, gifted with powerful wrists, hands and shoulders.

Ironically, it was fortunate that Mario's career began when it did—that is, during the arrival of the revolutionary rear-engined, lightweight racing car. Skill was a major factor with these cars, not pure stamina and brute strength. In long races the heavy roadster favored big men like Bryan, Foyt and Al Miller.

The new breed of racing cars also brought along a new breed of "compact" drivers; Jimmy Clark, Jackie Stewart, Gordon Johncock and, of course, Mario Andretti. Their modest size also provided a weight advantage which was not to be overlooked in the new era of "diet design" racing cars. Exotic metals such as titanium helped shed speed-consuming excess weight, as did the application of new thermoplastics. Most of the new body shells were fabricated of thin plastic or fiberglass, which, while being immensely strong, was lighter than the traditional aluminum.

Indianapolis 1965 saw a major turnover to the new look in cars, pioneered by Lotus, Lola and Brabham. The man who really started it all was England's John Cooper when he introduced the modern rear-engined car to the Grand Prix circuit.

For the most part, the United States Auto Club's old guard was not exactly

Placing second in the Hoosier Hundred to Foyt in 1965, Mario came back
to win this race the next two years in a row.

progressive. Brabham's underpowered Cooper—he was using a much smaller
Grand Prix engine—gave strong indications in 1961 of what was in the future.
Even in 1963, when Clark's Lotus almost won, many of the USAC "regulars"
resisted the change. In 1964 Parnelli Jones and A. J. Foyt elected to run
their faithful roadsters "one more time," even though both had tested and
driven Lotus Fords. Foyt's win that year was really a fluke, as mechanical
ills eliminated one faster rear-engined car after another.

But now it was 1965. Most of the entrants realized that the glorious roadster era was over. Both Jones and Foyt sported new Lotus cars. All but six
qualifiers were running rear-engined designs. Some were rather rough
imitations of Lotus and Lola.

But getting back to Mario and his new car. He had run it in some private
tests at the Brickyard before May. Having accumulated a wealth of information regarding suspension, Mario was instrumental in properly setting up the
new equipment.

Al Dean was a bit concerned about Andretti's debut. He had seen many
promising drivers blow their opportunity when the big moment arrived. Spend-
ing the entire month of May at Indianapolis is very tough on teams and
drivers. The pressure builds up, tempers flare. Many times when the big day
of qualifications arrives, some drivers just can't cut the mustard. Either the
car has been "overprepared" and won't run properly, or the driver is so up
tight that he spins out and muffs his chance for glory.

As it turned out, Dean's concern for Mario was groundless. He proved to
be devastatingly cool under pressure.

There was an interesting sidelight to the Brawner Brabham Hawk, Mario's new car. Clint had built the car with its engine set on the car's center line, not offset as in virtually all the other Indy cars. Colin Chapman, probably the most brilliant—though sometimes erratic—modern racing car designer in the world, had his engine off center in 1965, but had used center line positioning in 1964.

After extensive practicing, Mario was convinced the Brawner concept was the best for the quickest possible yet safe run for the "500." The Dean team had no illusions about having the fastest car, for it was obvious that Chapman had fresh innovations in the Clark car—which was backed by the Ford Motor Company—as did Foyt, Jones, Dan Gurney, Al Miller and Bobby Johns in theirs.

When the first qualification day arrived, with 200,000 looking on, Mario Andretti rolled out the white Hawk for his qualification attempt. A hush fell over the stands. The fans had not seen an Italian-born American driver since the great Ralph DePalma—and there were not many people left who had seen DePalma's exploits prior to World War I or even his American-born nephew, 1925 "500" winner, Peter DePaolo.

Mario cut four well-turned laps for a record average speed of 158.849. He was not to hold it long, for this year's classic qualifying battleground belonged to England's Jimmy Clark and super Texan A. J. Foyt. Clark rolled in with 160.729. But the cheers of the crowd had just barely died down when a determined Foyt hammered out four fresh laps which put him on the pole by a fraction, 161.233. Then Dan Gurney cut a set of laps which gave him the number three starting position.

So, within about thirty minutes, Mario had moved from the pole into the second row to fourth spot. But few rookies had qualified this well.

When it was all over, Mario stood quietly but confidently at his pit. Everyone was pleased with his initial time trial and he showed his assurance: "I know we've got the equipment. The car has a really good feel and I've never been readier for a fast ride. We'll soon find out if we're fast enough to take those Lotuses."

Mario also had something else going for him. An argument of some magnitude developed over a chunking problem with Goodyear tires. Foyt and other Goodyear-shod drivers suffered slightly from the use of a softer compound. This, by the way, caused a cautious Jimmy Clark to switch from Goodyear to Firestone during the practice session when the problem came up. But Mario was already on Firestone, so no trouble there.

When the field was finally set, it had one surprise. Rodger Ward didn't make it. He had all kinds of handling difficulties and the Watson-designed car just could not get up to the needed qualifying speed.

Then came Mario's big moment. There he was out on that world-famous

With the men who gave him his start in major league racing—the late Al Dean and Clint Brawner.

Mario Andretti

PERFECT CIRCLE

PREMIER

UNITED STATES AUTO CLUB 1965 REGISTERED CAR

AUTOLITE

grid in front of those giant stands. It's an awe-inspiring sight. But the young man was ready to go when Tony Hulman's traditional signal: "Gentlemen, start your engines!" was announced.

And start they did. The field of thirty-three cars made a perfect parade lap, then the pace car pulled into the pits and starter Pat Vidan whipped down the green flag. Like a flash, the dark green Lotus of Clark jumped out in front of A. J. Foyt, beating the Texas tiger into the first turn.

That was the basic battle of this "500," Clark and Foyt. But it became obvious that Clark was to be unbeatable. He also had the fabulous Wood Brothers as his pit crew. Indy fans were treated to the sight of a world's record for a pit stop—a full fuel load in 19.8 seconds!

Mario had started well, holding sixth position behind Clark, Foyt, Gurney, Jones and Miller at the end of the first ten laps, or twenty-five miles.

At the completion of twenty laps Andretti had slipped into fifth place ahead of Miller. On lap 43 Gurney dropped out due to broken timing gears, moving Mario into fourth.

He hung onto fourth spot through the 110th lap. The back of the Clark-Foyt contest was snapped when Foyt coasted into the pits with a broken transmission. The amazing rookie was now third!

Then began a battle for second spot between Andretti and veteran Parnelli Jones. The 1963 winner was having his hands full holding off an obviously determined Mario. With about twenty-five laps to go Jones found himself with a slim margin over the white Hawk Ford. Jones had to feed his engine carefully, as he was running low on fuel with two laps still to go. Twice Jones' car sputtered and appeared as though it would run dry. This was a battle which suddenly drew the fans' attention, as Clark had the race in the bag.

Jones began to weave his car back and forth across the track to suck up every ounce of go-juice left. By swishing the last drops of methanol into the fuel line, Jones was able to hold his thin margin and slip across the finish line six seconds ahead of the charging Mario Andretti. It was one of those Hollywood finishes, for after Jones crossed the line, his tank ran totally dry and the car stalled on the north end of the track. Parnelli pushed it the rest of the way into the pit area to the wild cheers of the standing crowd.

When Mario rolled into the pits, he too got a massive ovation for a tremendous drive. He was voted Rookie of the Year for the "500" and collected $42,551.

After the race, most of the afterhours talk was about Mario. One seasoned USAC official said, "Clark took the big money here today and he deserved it, but believe me, Andretti is the boy to watch from here on out."

The 1965 season continued and outside of the prestige-filled "500," one of the truly classic races on the Championship Trail was the Hoosier Grand Prix, the first USAC race to be run on a road course.

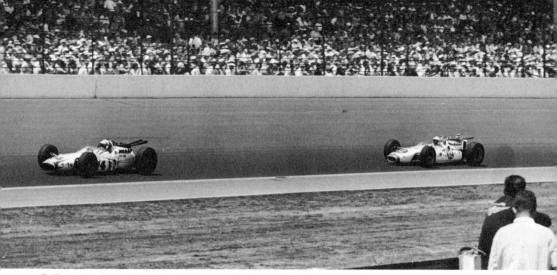

Following veteran Al Miller in the opening laps of the Indy "500,"
the amazing rookie quickly showed his ability when he passed
Miller for fifth place before twenty laps were gone.

Mario qualified the Hawk Ford at 111.626 mph. This placed him on the pole. The race itself turned out to be a tension-loaded contest between USAC's all-time ace, A. J. Foyt, and the young man on his way up, Mario Andretti. Again and again A. J. would lead on the straights, then Mario would snatch it back on the curves. Mario passed Foyt on the 79th lap for the final time, as the race ended on the 80th lap. It gave Mario his first victory on the Championship Trail. There would be many more to come.

Next was the Atlanta 250, in which Al Dean had Mario run the front-engined roadster. He qualified eighth and finished second. Then came the traditional Langhorne 125-miler. Still running the roadster, Andretti qualified third, but finished fourth. Back in the Hawk Ford for the Milwaukee 150, Mario was second on the grid and finished as he started, second.

At the Springfield 100, in the Dean dirt track car, he qualified sixth but managed to wind up third overall. Back at Milwaukee for the 200, Mario had the third best time, but mechanical problems dropped him to a sixteenth-place finish.

At DuQuoin, in September, back in the dirt car, Mario gridded seventh, but ended up fifteenth. However, at the famous Hoosier 100 dirt track race, he came in second. It would mark the first of many great contests there between Mario and A. J. Foyt.

Andretti wound up the 1965 season with a third at Sacramento and a second at the Phoenix 200. His steady season's performance brought Mario the 1965 National Championship. He earned a total of 3110 points, beating out defending champion A. J. Foyt who got 2500 and Jim McElreath who came in third with 2035.

For a young man in his first full year of major competition, Mario's performance was truly something remarkable.

A National Champion at Twenty-five

Not many men in USAC's brief history had become National Champions at the relatively young racing age of twenty-five. Even rarer were those who reached this pinnacle during their rookie year.

But it had become a fact of racing life that Mario Andretti was gifted with those rare talents that mark a champion. Not that he is superhuman, he'd make mistakes now and then, like overcooking it during a qualifying lap in an all-out try for the existing one-mile lap record. But over the long haul, Mario's page in the record book proves his consistency; another hallmark of a superb driver.

It was March and time for the first race of 1966 at Phoenix, where he had so deeply impressed the seasoned Arizona fans just about a year ago with a modified roadster.

Now he was back again, this time in the Hawk Ford which had served him well in 1965. Al Dean had always gone first class in supplying equipment for his team and drivers, so he decided to buy a Lotus chassis. It was picked up at the Los Angeles airport and hauled out to Dean's garage in Phoenix. Brawner and his crew spent hours setting up the Lotus, but for reasons which have not been made totally clear, the spanking new Lotus was never raced. Visitors at Firestone's open house prerace party at Indianapolis in 1966 saw the Lotus on display.

To prove a point, Mario took the Hawk out for some hot laps at the Speedway in December of 1965 after testing for Firestone. He had set a record lap of 164.1 mph. This substantiated Dean's thinking that Brawner had put together a car that was equal to the Lotus in performance.

So this is why Mario was running the Hawk once more. Again the fans were waiting for something spectacular from Andretti on the Phoenix track.

Foyt captured the pole position for the 1966 Hoosier Hundred and dueled with ▶
Andretti (nearer camera) for entire race, but Mario beat him to the checkered flag.

He didn't disappoint them. In qualifying Mario set a world record for a one-mile track of 122.075 mph. This put him on the pole.

When the race got going, Mario flashed out into the lead with A. J. Foyt riding shotgun. Suddenly they both spun out into the infield. After getting back into action, each was down two laps. Something had affected the Hawk, for Mario was forced out on the 48th lap with mechanical failure.

On April 24 USAC's Championship crowd ran at Trenton, as usual, the final event prior to the Brickyard trek on the 1st of May. Once again Mario showed the rest of the field the quickest way around the one-mile track, setting another qualifying record of 115.718. And again, he was on the pole. He ran a hard race, but finished fourth. Rodger Ward took the last checkered flag of his colorful career by winning this race. He would quit racing after the 1966 "500."

Then came the workout at Indianapolis in May. Mario, by the way, has never been overawed by this huge race plant. "Sure, it's a great race and the richest in the world," he explains, "but to me it's just another race track. I can think of two other Championship Trail tracks which I personally feel are much harder to race on. Then, of course, there are the really incredible circuits in Europe, like the Nürburgring. That's a really tough one. You have to learn 167 turns on a track that's fourteen miles long!

"There's a kind of mental block built up by some drivers that come here for the first time. You've got to realize that ten or fifteen years ago, Indy was a major challenge, as there were no other tracks in this country where you could drive as fast. But now with high speed banked places like Michigan, Daytona, Talledega and Ontario [California], Indy is not the total challenge it once was. Of course, the Five Hundred is a classic event to be in and it has an atmosphere like no other place in the world.

"You may remember that Jim Clark shook up the old timers there when he flew back and forth to Europe for his Grand Prix races. This is a way of life for the Formula One guys. To them the Five Hundred was just another race, and they were not putting it down.

"With the racing schedule becoming so crowded these days and drivers running other events besides their own series—such as I've been doing—the Indy people will be forced to cut down on the time spent there. I suppose it's a ball to those guys who have nothing else to do all month."

Everything appeared to be going nicely for Mario as he prepared for his second "500." The Hawk was running well.

There was some fresh competition from the Grand Prix ranks. A young up-and-coming Scotsman, Jackie Stewart, came in to drive millionaire sportsman John Mecom's Lola Ford. A veteran GP champion, Englishman Graham Hill, was assigned Mecom's other car, the American Red Ball Special. From NASCAR came a bright stock car ace, Cale Yarborough.

Many slow laps after the first lap crash at Indy
contributed to Mario's engine failure and early retirement.

When the tense initial weekend of qualifications was over—this is when the hot shoes all try for the pole—Mario Andretti had sewed up the coveted number one position with a high mark of 165.899. Jim Clark got the second spot while George Snider, in Foyt's team car, completed the front row. Foyt had racked up his car during practice and was forced to qualify the second weekend.

At the start of the race when the command to turn it on was given after the pace lap, Mario had brought the field of thirty-three cars around in what appeared to be a smooth start. Coming down the main straight, all hell broke loose.

One car faltered and triggered a mass pileup of closely knit cars. Snapped off wheels were flying in all directions. During the wild confusion, Foyt leaped out of his wrecked car and set some kind of fence climbing record as he scrambled out of the way. The race had to be red flagged. The debris made it impossible for the lead cars, including Andretti, to come around and get through.

When the smoke had cleared and the biggest used car mess in American racing history swept off the track, eleven cars had been knocked out of the race, including Foyt, Gurney, Yarborough and Miller. Through some miracle, no one was injured.

After slightly more than an hour, the "500" was restarted. Almost at once, after the green, Johnny Boyd whacked the wall, bringing out the slow speed yellow flag. Following the 17th lap, the green came on again and as Andretti socked it to his throttle, ominous smoke was seen pouring from his car's exhaust as he went through the first turn.

On the back stretch Clark whipped by the white Hawk. It was obvious that Mario was in trouble. Then he was black flagged twice before pulling reluctantly into the pits. Back out Mario went, but after only one lap, he was back in with valve trouble. The Dean crew worked frantically on the ailing car, but to no avail. It was retired after twenty-seven laps. So a frustrated Andretti was a spectator as a somewhat surprised Graham Hill went on to win.

After the race, Mario told a reporter: "When I put my foot in after the yellow, it was like sticking my foot in a bowl of Jello."

Somebody asked why he hadn't kept going, even on seven cylinders. Mario said: "What would be the point? I couldn't possibly finish, let alone win. Plus the danger of blowing a $25,000 engine and endangering the rest of the field."

Mario appeared to be haunted by the hex that had plagued many previous USAC National Champions; they could not beg, borrow or steal a win at the biggest race of all, Indianapolis.

However, Andretti set aside his misfortunes and concentrated upon the remainder of the season.

With perhaps a deep desire to show that his car did have the potential to

◀ At Langhorne he set a world mile record and led the race from flag to flag.

win, Mario went to Milwaukee, set a fresh qualifying record to sit on the pole and led the 100-miler from start to finish.

Then came the 100-miler at the always tough Langhorne track. Again Andretti set still another world mile record. On the pole, he led from flag to flag for his second straight victory.

Once again the Indy cars invaded the deep South, running on the high banked NASCAR track at Atlanta. This time it was a 300-miler. A large field of thirty cars qualified. Mario seemed unbeatable as he set another track record, qualifying at 169.014. He went on to win, the only driver to complete the full 200 laps.

At the Hoosier Grand Prix, a 150-miler, run on the one-and-seven-eighths-mile road course, Lloyd Ruby sat on the pole, but it was Mario who took the checkered flag. He now had won four straight Trail events.

The USAC traveling company came back to Langhorne. Mario, in his eagerness to break his own records, whacked the wall on his second qualifying lap. Ironically, he did set a record on the first lap, but was unable to drive the Hawk in the race itself. He got another ride in one of the Jim Robbins cars, but could only finish twenty-first.

Moving to Springfield for another dirt track 100-miler, the late Don Branson, a canny dirt track man, outfoxed Mario to lead him across the finish line. Foyt was third, his best finish so far, as A. J. was having a miserable season, the worst of his career.

But at the Milwaukee 200 in August Mario had everything going for him, as he took the pole position and the race. Another dirt track go at DuQuoin found Andretti unable to finish.

Then came the rich, classic Hoosier 100, a dirt track masterpiece. Foyt virtually "owned" this track. To no one's surprise A. J. drew the pole, but as for the race itself, the packed stands were treated to a great battle royal as Foyt and Andretti dueled back and forth during the entire 100 miles. Mario managed to slip by A. J. and take the checker.

Back at Trenton for the 200-miler, Mario once more demonstrated his mastery by setting another record, a winning race average for 200 miles of 105.127. At Sacramento, the dirt track bug jumped up again and Mario wound up tenth.

It might be interesting to insert a note here about the dirt track scene. Clint Brawner points out why running on the clay tracks was not Mario's strong racing skill: "Jimmy Bryan, who drove our Dean cars, was, without question, the greatest dirt track man I've ever seen.

"But you must consider the fact that there were more dirt races than there are now. Take A. J. Foyt. He's run many more of these races than has Mario. With the expanded schedule we have now, more road races, plus the new tracks like Michigan and Dover, we have time to run maybe three or four dirt track races in a season."

Brawner also feels that dirt track racing isn't what it once was—the gutsy, no-holds-barred scene that brought fans probably the most spine-tingling brand of oval racing.

Says Brawner: "Dirt racing is a bum show these days. Before, the track was rough and we could run them the same way. The tracks used to be wet down more, but now the promoters want them hard and slick, so the drivers don't tear up the track and throw a lot of clay around or get the crowd dusty. It's a bad show when you can't run as hard as you are capable of doing, because the track is just too slick. Take Nazareth, for example, even Mario doesn't want to run it, even though it's his home track."

For the final race of the season at Phoenix, Mario wound up his tremendous performance in 1966 by again taking the pole and also winning this 200-miler.

Thus he enjoyed a fantastic season, winning eight out of fifteen Championship races, which brought Mario his second straight USAC National Championship. It was a good year.

However, 1967 would be something different.

Mario's face shows an expression of distaste—a natural reaction to the heavily nitro-laden fumes as the crew helps him start his engine.

His first NASCAR stock car race was the 1966 Firecracker 400 in the Cotton Owens Dodge #5. He was challenging the leaders when his engine blew. Here he's leading second place finisher Darel Dieringer (16) and Paul Goldsmith.

Here, There and Everywhere in Racing

This racing season would be a mixed bag for Mario. He started 1967 off with an impact that NASCAR won't forget for many years to come.

Andretti agreed to take a whack at running the Daytona 500, wheeling a red and gray Ford Fairlane prepped by the wizards of stock car magic, Holman and Moody.

Now to the good old boys on the Southern circuit, the Daytona 500-mile yearly ritual is every bit as important and prestige-filled as the Indianapolis "500" is to the Championship mob.

A. J. Foyt had shaken up some of the stock car faithful by snatching the Firecracker 400 at the Big D; however, *nobody*, but *nobody* from outside the NASCAR ranks had ever gone back up to damn-Yankee country with the big bag of boodle one can grab at the Daytona 500.

So here comes this little guy, who looks like a lost waif alongside guys like Darel Dieringer, Junior Johnson, Curtis Turner and Buddy Baker.

Even race-wise Ronney Householder, the tough mandarin who cracks the directional whip for Chrysler, was not impressed with Mario Andretti. Householder reacted the way Andy Granatelli once did when Mario sought a ride in one of his thundering Novis. No dice.

"Mario Andretti? No chance," bluntly asserted Householder. "It takes a strong man to handle these stock cars on a track like this. He's just too small for this kind of traffic. Did you see how high he was running in the hundred-miler? He couldn't hold the car on the track."

Well, Ronney was wrong. But everybody is, now and then. While qualifying, Mario was good but not earth-shaking. He turned in a two-lap average of 177.444. But the real froster for this clambake was the Babe Ruth of stock

No match for Darel Dieringer in size, Andretti quickly proved that size isn't everything by winning the 1967 Daytona 500.

Defending his title at Riverside in the last race of 1967, a late pit stop
for fuel dropped him to third place and gave the Championship to Foyt.

car racing, Curtis Turner. Chrysler and Ford people were unhinged when
Turner put Smokey Yunick's Chevelle on the pole. Turner chopped a pair
of quickies for a record average of 180.831. Mario's time was eclipsed by
Richard Petty, Foyt, Dieringer, Cale Yarborough and LeeRoy Yarbrough.
However, it was reported that Mario shook up the locals when he later turned
in a practice lap of over 182 mph.

When the giant field roared off down the main straight, Turner stomped
on it and led for the first lap. At forty-three he proved his point. Then he
eased off to let the young lions have a go at it.

During the early laps, young Buddy Baker was out front, tailed by David
Pearson, Yarbrough, Foyt, Turner, Dieringer—and outrider Mario Andretti.

Later Mario cited his game: "During those early laps, I was more or less

After beating back a strong challenge from Jim Hall's Chaparral,
Andretti and Bruce McLaren captured the 12 Hours of Sebring.

spectating. I think I could have been up in there, but when a race like this is
five hundred miles long, there is plenty of time to make a decisive move."

When the yellow came out on the 24th lap, the NASCAR leaders all
whipped into the pits. But Mario kept rolling, with Paul Goldsmith riding his
bumper. When the green was flashed, Goldsmith jumped in front. Andretti
just as quickly took it back.

Mario was betting on another yellow for a much needed fuel stop. He got
it when Goldsmith crunched the wall. After tanking up, Mario was but a few
spots off the pace. He regained the lead very shortly.

The big two-and-a-half-mile oval was now getting oily and cars began falling out right and left. This brought on the yellow each time and the good old
boys were having a tough time trying to overhaul the USAC Champion. Don

White was pouring oil. Then Foyt broke his flywheel. LeeRoy's engine blew. Petty was in various kinds of trouble.

On lap 120 Baker blew his engine. Finally Turner's overworked Chevelle lunched its engine. Then fifteen laps later Pearson separated his power plant.

At this point, Mario and Ford master driver Freddy Lorenzen were having a great dog fight. Again the yellow was unfurled. Andretti and Lorenzen pitted for fuel. Freddy got out first.

Then Mario got out in front once more, swinging his Fairlane up high coming through the turns. In turn four he seemed to take up almost two lanes, which disturbed the NASCAR boys. It seems Mario likes to run a stocker with loose suspension, so he lets it all hang out.

Lorenzen by now was playing his famous drafting game to save fuel. He must have thought that Mario wouldn't have the go-power to get too far in front. But he was wrong.

In the final ten laps Mario put his foot in it. He was running as though this were a 100-miler. He widened his lead to six seconds, and that's the way it was to the checker.

Andretti thus became the first USAC, and non-NASCAR driver, to win Bill France's racing pearl.

"This had to be the toughest race I've ever driven," said a tired Mario in the press box. "The physical pounding on the banking and the degree of concentration running those speeds took a lot out of me."

There was one humorous footnote to the Daytona victory. The Firestone clan was on hand and Kate Firestone got her first look at Mario and said, "Look at him! He's so teensy!" With a wry followup, the *Detroit News* racing reporter wrote, "He's toughsy and fastsy, too."

Next on Mario's busy schedule was another deal for Ford; he would again drive a Mark IV sports car at Sebring's rough 12-hour endurance go in March.

He had had bad luck at Sebring in 1966. Mario was running a Ferrari when his gears locked up on a corner. He spun and collided with a Porsche. The Porsche went off the pavement and scaled into a cluster of people who were standing in a no-spectator area. Several were killed. Then, to top off the tragedy, when he drove back to the pits, Mario's machine caught fire.

Ford was very high on Andretti, which it should be. Mario had won two straight USAC National Championships with Ford power and had copped the Daytona 500 for them.

Therefore he was asked to share a Ford GT at Sebring with Bruce McLaren. Ford was thirsting for this classic road race, as they had been bombed out of the ball park at Daytona by Ferrari in February. So they mounted a pair of new Mark IVs—an update of the earlier J-car.

Andretti's major competition was expected to be from Jim Hall's very quick

Fresh from his victory at Sebring, he blew a tire while passing
leader Cale Yarborough in the Atlanta 500.

new Chaparral. Supplying top flight support was the fine pairing of A. J. Foyt
and Lloyd Ruby in a Mark II Ford.

Still a spine tingler, though somewhat outmoded, is the 60-car field getting
off from a Le Mans start. Somehow a mass crunch is always avoided, as everything from seven-liter monsters to mosquito Sprites steam down the wide
track that was once a runway for World War II bombers.

By the time the first hour had passed, the superb combination of Andretti
and McLaren had finished twenty laps. Running second was the Mark II of
Foyt/Ruby. On the initial fuel stop it was discovered that eleven gallons of
the vital forty-two needed to top up were not getting into the tank. This might
mean an extra pit stop. So Andretti was ordered to pick up the pace to allow
for such an emergency.

But the Chaparral was moving just as quickly. After the third hour, while
in the pits, McLaren was passed by Hall. Then they reversed positions when
Hall pitted.

The whole twelve hours turned out to be a Ford-Chaparral contest. But
later the Chaparral went out with electrical failure.

Andretti and McLaren sailed on to victory, with Foyt barely taking second
due to a fantastically long pit stop.

1967 marked the second year in a row that Mario had captured
Indy's pole position only to drop out early in the race.

A. J. Foyt (at left rear tire) helps Mario and his crew push his car off the track after crashing in practice prior to the 200-miler at Mosport.

Mario hardly had enough time to kiss his wife and gulp a bit of bubbly, before Ford's racing people stuffed Foyt and Andretti into a private plane and hustled them off to run the Atlanta 500 stock car race the very next afternoon.

Having just run a twelve-hour grind this, perhaps, was not the wisest of moves, taking on a tough high speed stock car race with little or no rest.

Foyt and Lorenzen staged a great battle until Foyt's engine blew. With only thirteen hours between climbing out of a Mark IV and strapping himself into a Fairlane, Andretti worked his way up through the field—he had started in twenty-second position—much in the manner of a Roman legion. By the 140th lap he was setting his sights for leader Cale Yarborough. Then these two ran as though no one else was on the track. On lap 152 Mario dove down under Cale and got by. The lead was switched a half dozen times.

Going by Cale once again, Mario blew a tire, whacking the retaining wall. Pitting, the crew unbent the sheet metal and replaced the tires. Getting back into combat, Andretti was two laps down.

He blew still another tire when his brakes locked up during a pit stop. Going back out, Mario was frustrated to find his steering was out of alignment. He then parked it for good.

One thing for sure, the Southern fans discovered this little guy from up North could wheel a stocker along with the best that NASCAR had. If they thought he was lucky at Daytona, he proved his point at Atlanta.

However, some of the NASCAR boys were not too happy with Mario's all-out driving. "I guess I'm just scared of him," commented Richard Petty. "You can't get too close to him. He'll run right over you in the turns or down the straights."

One other NASCAR driver commented, "I guess after driving those cars he's used to, getting in a stock car must be like driving a tank."

Of course, the good old boys were glad to have Cale win that Atlanta 500 and crack the winning streak of those pesky USAC aliens from Yankeeland. Parnelli Jones had captured the season-opener at Riverside, Andretti had won Daytona and the defending champion at Atlanta was Jim Hurtubise.

Now it was time for Mario to turn to his first and most important racing love, Championship competition.

Again Clint Brawner decided to stay with a winning design, his Brabham Hawk. Little changes were incorporated, but basically it was the same car that brought Mario his 1966 driving title.

However, Brawner, Andretti and the rest of the USAC boys would soon be getting the automotive shock of their racing careers in the form of something called a *turbine*.

In April it was a lost cause at the season-opener, as Mario mashed his car in practice and could not even qualify. Foyt was fifth.

At Trenton the old Mario magic was working well. He took the pole and won without too much trouble.

Now it was time to trek to Tony Hulman's grand arena for "The Race." But this year's "500" would foment more argument, more controversy and get more publicity than any other race in Indianapolis history—it might also be safe to add, any race ever run.

USAC had agreed to okay the now feared and hated silent screamer, the STP Turbocar. The word had quickly spread to all that this car would be unbeatable, a fact which grew like Topsy as the practice days rolled by in May. The car was a marvel of control. Its four-wheel-drive gave Parnelli Jones solid assurance no matter what line he took through the corners.

Mario and his crew set to work, regardless. Fitted with the latest version of the turbocharged Ford engine, the Hawk moved easily around the big oval.

The Trenton 200 was the turning point in the Championship battle between Andretti and Foyt. After capturing the pole position, Mario (above) pulled away from Foyt (14) only to tangle with Lloyd Ruby later in the race and crash (below).

8

On his way to victory in the Daytona 500. Here he's leading
former NASCAR ace Freddie Lorenzen, who finished second.

Nothing could stay with him, not even the turbine. But then people were saying that Jones was sandbagging, not running at full power.

So the first big qualifying day came. It was after four o'clock when Mario went to cast his four laps. Some of the corners were a little slippery. The pressure was really on. Many had predicted a 170-mile lap this year, including Andretti himself. First Joe Leonard cracked Mario's 1966 record. Then Dan Gurney banged out a 167.224 mph average, edging Leonard.

Now it was up to Mario. His first lap: 169.205, a record. The second lap was a whisker slower: 169.014. His third lap was up: 169.779. The fourth one would have to be it.

But fates of racing ruled otherwise. He boggled slightly in turn one, and almost lost it in turn three. Mario cooled it through four, using his head. So he came up with a 167.942. He had the pole, but at an average of 168.982.

Later Mario admitted: "It was just too slippery. I almost wiped it out in the third turn, so rather than wreck, I played it safe. I wanted that 170-mph record, but not by wrecking my car."

Parnelli Jones was said to be having gearbox loading trouble, thus he had to settle for a 166.075 average. But had things gone as everyone thought they would, Jones could have started last and still wiped out the field.

Back in the garage area, Mario was quietly resigned to the seeming fact that everybody would be battling for second place behind Jones. "There is no way, but *no* way I can beat that damn thing if it stays together. Parnelli can run it all day at 165 or more. Well, I'm going to go as hard as I can."

The fifty-first running of the "500" was packed full of surprises. Most of them are, but this one was in a class by itself. This car was the story itself!

As the thirty-three cars took Pat Vidan's green flag, it looked like a smooth, conventional race. Diving into turn one came Andretti, Johncock, Gurney and Foyt in a ballet line. Then the classic racing bubble burst. Whipping to the *outside* of the first turn, Parnelli shot past three of the confident front runners as though they were glued. Coming out of turn two, Jones and the bright red silent screamer ducked *under* Andretti and flashed into the lead going down the back stretch.

Parnelli, right on the first lap, was making this race look like a child's game. He had absolute control over the other thirty-two cars.

Cars began to fall out. Then suddenly Mario's car slipped into the pits. Was he done? It seemed so. His clutch was gone. So he couldn't care less about that damned turbine now.

But this drama was about to take another turn. Huge heavy clouds had hung over the packed racing plant all morning. Then they let loose. It didn't stop, so the race did. For the first time since 1915, the "500" was postponed until the following day.

Andretti had won a reprieve. The clutch was replaced. He could continue.

Clint Brawner and his crew were happy for the rain at Indy,
as it gave them time to repair the clutch in Mario's car while it sat
in the pits under a sea of umbrellas and plastic sheets.

But his chances of winning were slim. He was too far behind. If he placed in the first ten, he'd be fortunate.

So he socked it to the Hawk, driving as hard as he could, the absolute limit. In traffic he turned one lap at 166 mph! His competitive spirit is such that he just can't sandbag. It was all or nothing.

Jones continued to mount a giant lead. Gurney, who had run hard to stay behind him, finally dropped out with a burned piston. Now A. J. Foyt played the cat and mouse game, moving into second spot.

With chilling suddenness, Mario's right front wheel flew off. His built-in skill prevented a near collision, and he steered the crippled Hawk into the infield.

Mario's "Indy Jinx" had struck again. But no one would ever feel the frustration, the sickening agony of defeat which struck Parnelli Jones three laps from glory and automotive history. A broken six-dollar bearing sent him coasting into the pits and an unbelieving 250,000 fans watched a wildly happy A. J. Foyt take the winner's flag.

Back in the garage area, a disappointed, but determined Andretti said, "I'm not giving up. We'll just have to try harder next year. I'll win this race one day."

He was making an accurate prediction, but this would mean waiting longer than he had planned. Even with his unhappy finish, his efforts paid off with $21,048.

Back on the Championship Trail, Mario was unable to qualify for the Milwaukee 150 because of an accident in practice, and at Langhorne, he encountered more difficulty. He qualified sixth and ended up third.

Then Ford asked Mario to run a big GT at the grueling 24 Hours of Le Mans. This venture nearly cost him his life.

Ford was determined to repeat at Le Mans. If you include two Ford-powered Mirages and a Shelby Mustang, there were thirteen Fords on the line! Ferrari had ten entries all told.

The most formidable pairing was that of A. J. Foyt and Dan Gurney. Foyt had never been there, but within a few laps he was going full bore in practice.

After the race started, things looked good for Ford. They were dominating the scene. Then disaster struck during the small hours of Sunday morning.

Lucian Bianchi, paired with Mario, had been running in second place. He whipped into the pits for a routine replacement of brake pads and a driver change.

Mario jumped in and off he went. Going into the tricky esses, he braked as usually required. The brakes locked up, spinning his Ford backward into the earth embankment and then out onto the track. Dazed, but not injured, it took a brief period—which must have seemed an eternity—before Mario could extricate himself.

By a fateful coincidence, coming at full bore in another Ford was Roger McCluskey. Seeing the crippled Andretti car, McCluskey spun his Mark II to avoid the helpless Andretti and, in turn, clobbered the banking. The French officials, displaying their usual talent for lack of common sense, had not yet put out a yellow flag. To cap this weird plot, still another Ford came bearing down on the cluttered area. It was Jo Schlesser. Using all the skill he had to miss the two Fords, he crashed. No one was injured, but the Ford people back in the pits were standing around in a state of shock when they learned that three major entries had been wiped out within minutes!

Mario finally got back to the pits, tired and sore from the safety harness.

One is reminded of an interview Mario gave before he went to Le Mans that year: "I'd like to have one good memory from Le Mans. Then I'd quit it for sure. I'd like to say I enjoy this race, but I don't. It's tremendously dangerous. There are no safety features to speak of. If you are caught in a fire at Le Mans, tough luck."

Needless to say, Mario has no plans to go back there after that nightmare. As it turned out, Ford would not return either. For in a petty attempt to restrict the American racing effort, the FIA, the French ruling body of racing, reduced the engine size to three liters for 1968.

Despite the debacle of losing three cars, Foyt and Gurney stayed out in front of the stalking Ferraris and Porsches to capture Ford's second straight Le Mans victory.

Returning to the U.S., Mario took his Hawk to Mosport for the USAC 200-miler run over the difficult twisting road course. The gremlins were still hanging on as on the very first lap, after starting in fifteenth position, Mario snapped a half shaft. After repairs, he was back in the race after lap 38, but it was too late.

In the second 100-mile heat, Mario demonstrated his great road racing talent by setting the highest speed of the day: 178 mph, which was also the highest speed ever recorded at Mosport. Then the rains came, shortening the rather dismal—at least for Andretti—race. He wound up eleventh in the second heat. Foyt finished seventh in both heats.

However, at Indianapolis Raceway Park everything fell into place for Mario. He qualified second and won the 150-miler. Seventh place went to Foyt.

It was obvious now that the 1967 Championship fight would be between Mario and A. J., but now Andretti would have to scratch hard, as A. J. had the fat 1000 points from winning Indy.

At Langhorne it was two straight. Gordon Johncock set a world record for a mile track and got the pole, but Mario picked up 300 important Championship points by winning. Then another Canadian road race was on the docket at St. Jovite. Run in two 100-mile heats, Mario was superb there.

The Andretti/Bianchi big Ford GT was running in second place
at Le Mans when a brake malfunction caused it to crash.

He won both heats, but Foyt was in there too. He came in second both times. It was quite a road show between USAC's top drivers.

At Springfield it was another one of those tense dirt track battles between Mario and A. J., who managed to edge out Andretti, and they finished in that order.

Back at Milwaukee Mario turned it on and swept this 200-miler, picking up another 400 valuable points, as Foyt wound up eighth. DuQuoin saw another storybook Foyt-Andretti contest. Once again it was A. J.'s turn, with Mario winding up a close second.

Then the very rich and unmatched Hoosier 100. A packed grandstand watched Foyt and Andretti renew their now classic rivalry. After endless lead swaps, Mario got around Foyt to take his second straight victory there.

The Trenton 200 proved to be a break for Foyt. Mario was on the pole and had moved out in front with little difficulty. Ruby set out with total determination, whipping past Foyt. On lap five he caught Mario and tried to dive under the Hawk but Mario clung to his line. In racing lingo, he had closed the door, shut the gate on Ruby, which is fair in love, war and auto racing. Ruby was trapped and the two collided after Ruby spun. Both cars were knocked out. So Mario had to sit by helplessly while Foyt stormed on to win.

Back at Sacramento Foyt and Andretti had at it again on the dirt and Mario did his best, but A. J. on dirt is rough. They finished on the same lap, but Foyt was in front again.

The possibilities for Mario repeating his Championship were dimming fast. Now it began to look really dark. At the Hanford 200 Mario tangled with Al Unser and was eliminated. Foyt lost out to Johncock, coming in fourth, but he had picked up more points. Foyt now had 3280 points to Andretti's 2540.

At Phoenix in November Mario pulled the point pendulum the other way, winning the 200-miler while Foyt went out after ninety-two laps.

Now came the moment of truth for the two contenders seeking the prestige-filled USAC National Championship; the Rex Mays 300. The winner there would pick up 600 points.

Well, to make it quick and to the point, Mario was frustrated in his hopes there by two factors; running low on fuel and a USAC rule which permitted car hopping. The first factor gave Dan Gurney the victory; the second gave the 1967 Championship to A. J. Foyt.

Mario appeared to have the race bagged when he was forced to pit for enough fuel—six gallons—in order to finish the race. He had but *six* laps to go. Mario had taken the lead when Gurney had to pit with a cut tire.

Foyt was having his hangups as well. He had brought a backup car just in case. With Hurtubise driving, it sprang an oil leak and had to be retired during

Mario's wife, DeeAnn, joins him on the hood of his Ford Fairlane in Daytona's Victory Circle. ▶

the early part of the race. Almost at the same time, Foyt had to go off course to avoid the spinning car of Al Miller. A. J. ran a half-mile back to the pits. Finding his backup car out, Goodyear had "arranged" a deal with Roger McCluskey to turn his car over to A. J. After a hectic cockpit alteration, Foyt stormed out only to return pointing to the fuel filler cap. An errant crewman had forgotten to close it. Out he went once more, only to find Mario ten seconds ahead.

Even after Mario saw his victory hopes vanish with his low fuel supply, Foyt again was in trouble. A rear half shaft had broken. He had to limp around in order to finish, which he did in fifth place.

The final point split between McCluskey and Foyt gave A. J. just the edge he needed.

The point score for 1967: Foyt 3440; Andretti 3360. He had lost out by a mere 80 points!

Actually, Mario had enjoyed a pretty good year. He had won eight Championship races, plus Daytona and Sebring.

There was a pleasant ending for Mario Andretti that season. He was voted Driver of the Year by Martini and Rossi, and was awarded $7500 and a beautiful bronze trophy.

In December, however, the Dean team was saddened by the passing of its founder, Al Dean, who died from a slow increase of cancer. He had given much to racing and, of course, had put Mario on the road to glory.

It was decided that Mario would take over the Dean racing stable and Clint Brawner and Jim McGee would carry on as his co-chief mechanics.

So now, it was time to get ready for the 1968 season. Perhaps this would be the year for Mario at Indianapolis.

A Study in Frustration

For reasons one can never properly explain, the fates of racing elected to look the other way when Mario Andretti launched his 1968 season. Not that he had a poor season. But by his exceptionally high levels of success, it was *not* a good year. However, all but a couple of USAC drivers would have gladly settled for Mario's racing fortunes.

The Andretti team was able to secure a rather unusual, but enthusiastic sponsor for '68, Overseas National Airways. Its young president was a racing buff, which accounts, in the main, for the involvement.

While Clint Brawner was busy setting up a revised and improved Hawk for the Championship Trail, Ford nominated Mario to run the Riverside 500 in January.

Andretti qualified eighth. During the long grind itself, the lead was changed frequently. After a quarter of an hour of hectic competition, Mario got into fourth position; eventually he got by Dan Gurney who was then third. Following a flurry of pit stops, Andretti and David Pearson shared the front spot. But after an hour and twenty minutes of hot competition, Mario was sidelined with a dropped valve.

The always restless young man then elected to run at Daytona's tough 24 Hours of Endurance. As Ford had officially withdrawn from factory competition due to the new displacement restrictions, Mario teamed up with Lucien Bianchi to run a promising Alfa T33 three-liter sports prototype. They qualified well, eleventh. The potent new factory Porsches virtually ran away with the enduro, but Mario and Bianchi brought their Alfa in sixth overall.

Ford signed Mario again for the always tough Daytona 500 NASCAR race. With all the hot dogs running hard, Andretti worked his way up in his usual charging manner and he was soon running third.

On lap 53 Mario took command. Cale Yarborough snaked through and snatched the lead on lap 88, building up a two-second cushion. Suddenly Mario appeared to lose it on lap 104. He and Buddy Baker slammed together. Sliding backward, he spun his Mercury around and went to the pits. That was it for Daytona 1968.

In early March Mario went to Indianapolis to run tire tests for Firestone.

A dejected Andretti slumps exhaustedly in the press room along with
race winner Dan Gurney (right) and new Champion Bobby Unser. For the
second year in a row the Rex Mays 300 had cost him the USAC title.

The bizarre sequence of events that cost Mario the USAC National Driving Championship in the final race of 1968 began when his engine failed while leading. He loosens his chin strap as he heads down the pits. . . .

◀ Parnelli Jones meets him and counsels with Mario as they stride
toward the end pit where Joe Leonard will be called in. . . .

As Leonard tells Andretti that the brakes are low, Parnelli puts a seat
cushion in the cockpit so that Mario can reach the pedals (Note Andy and
Vince Granatelli watching intently at extreme left of picture). . . .

After the demise of both Turbocars, Parnelli picked up Mario and they cycle down the pits, searching for another ride. . . .

Finally Mario gets Lloyd Ruby's car and makes ready to return to the race. Andretti moved the car up from fourth to third by the end, but to no avail as he lost the Championship by a mere eleven points.

He drove his new turbocharged Brawner Hawk Ford, cutting easy laps in the 160s. This car was lighter than the '67 Hawk which, according to Mario, had "improved braking, acceleration and cornering and was almost three miles an hour quicker than last year."

Mario also predicted it would take 173 mph to lock up the pole for the "500."

Going to Hanford, California for the opening Championship Trail race, title contenders Foyt and Andretti had assorted hangups, which resulted in Gordon Johncock winning. Mario was forced out with a broken half shaft; however defending USAC Champion Foyt finished fourth.

As the factory Alfas elected to skip Sebring, so did Mario, and in the meantime those turbines would be back at Indy, as Jimmy Clark had given the new Lotus turbine a shakedown run. There would be perhaps three, all running under the STP banner.

For the first time the Championship cars ran a 150-miler on the Stardust Raceway, just outside Las Vegas. Here Mario suffered one of the most irritating losses of his career. He and Bobby Unser had a great duel going into the final laps, when Mario was forced to pit for fuel five laps from the checker. That brief pause gave Bobby Unser the flag by a scant two seconds over Mario. His Ford had more go-power than Bobby's Offy, but it appears Mario's engine was sucking up more fuel.

Mario was now under some pressure as Phoenix came up. He had done well here before and it was expected that he and veteran Lloyd Ruby would put on a real show. As it was, both Mario and Bobby Unser were sitting on the front row, with Bobby on the pole. After twenty-three laps of racing, Mario got by the hard-charging Unser and opened up some daylight. Suddenly Roger McCluskey got by Mario on lap 47. On lap 80 Al Unser blew his engine, triggering a three-car crash, which included Mario. He was really in trouble for the '68 title, as Bobby Unser was taking the flags.

The jinx didn't let up at Trenton in April, where Mario had won twice quite handily. But Bobby Unser had a hot streak going which was not to be denied. He won his third straight, with Mario coming once more only two seconds down. It was obvious now that it would not be Foyt's year. Perhaps Bobby Unser would be the guy Mario was going to have to worry about.

It was *that* time again, the annual trek to the Brickyard. This year tensions would be somewhat more relaxed than last year. The turbines had been reduced in power, but the worry wart still plagued drivers. Andy Granatelli had sued the United States Auto Club to have his original Turbocar legalized. He lost.

This race was a blend of strange happenings. First, Granatelli had lost the services of the brilliant Jimmy Clark, who had lost his life in a tragic, mysterious accident in Germany in April. As things turned out, Joe Leonard was

In the Telegram Trophy at Mosport Mario (2) finished second
to winner Dan Gurney (48) in both hundred-mile races.

After practice at Monza for the 1968 Italian Grand Prix, Bobby Unser
and Mario climb aboard a helicopter to begin their journey back to the
United States for the Hoosier Hundred.

nominated to drive one of the Turbocars, as Parnelli Jones said he would
sit this one out for reasons that were clouded in a rash of assorted stories.
Graham Hill had the second STP Turbocar while Art Pollard's name seemed
to come out of an unlikely hat for the third silent screamer.

Mario was busy shaking down his new Hawk. He was confident that he
could do it this time, despite the Turbocars. He had plenty of power. The
only hangup might be fuel consumption.

When the big day of qualifying was finished, probably the most chagrined
driver at the Brickyard was Mario Andretti. Joe Leonard got the pole with
a sparkling 171.559 mph, while Graham Hill was slightly slower for the second spot. But what galled Mario was that Bobby Unser was extracting speeds
from his turbo Offy which were not thought possible.

Acknowledging the checkered flag with his hand raised in the air, he crosses ▶
the finish line after winning both heats of the Labatt 200 at St. Jovite. ▶

Unser became the first to crack the 170 mark with a piston engine. Almost pushed into the background was Mario. He cut an average of 168.982 mph. Even with his more powerful engine, he couldn't clip the magic 170 mark.

So Mario had to settle for fourth position. But that would not be his largest blow. The fates were saving the miserable treatment for the big race itself.

Two Turbocars were knocked out by a strange mechanical lapse once again as sure victory seemed within grasp. Graham Hill had crashed after losing a wheel. But the man whose pride really was shattered was Mario Andretti. He had to settle for an ignominious thirty-third finish.

On the very first lap, as he was gearing up to go after Leonard who had snatched the lead from the flag, Mario's ill-fated engine broke. Then in a last minute, desperate attempt to make the scene—somehow, anyhow—Mario unseated Larry Dickson from his backup car, but that engine blew shortly after he got out on the track.

What made it even tougher was that Bobby Unser won. This gave the all-out charger four straight races! It appeared as if Bobby had the '68 title bagged.

Not unlike a star ball player in a slump, it now seemed that Mario could not buy a victory. At Milwaukee, where this race was marred by a flaming accident which claimed the life of veteran Ronnie Duman, Lloyd Ruby finally got the flag, with Mario at least coming in second. This time Bobby Unser failed to finish. But Bobby had 2100 points, while Andretti was buried in fifth position with only a mere 720.

At Mosport, Canada, Mario displayed his tremendous technique at road racing. He was up against Dan Gurney, who knew this difficult road course better than anyone entered.

Gurney won both 100-mile heats, but Mario hung in there to finish second twice to USAC's best road runner. Unser, pressing too hard, crashed in the first heat and of course did not start the second, so Mario picked up more valuable points.

But the luck abruptly changed at Langhorne, normally a good track to Mario. "Snake bit" again, Andretti could not cut it this time, ending up seventeenth after falling out on the 44th lap. When the accident-marred 150-miler was done, Gordon Johncock had posted the win, with Bobby Unser second, picking up more points.

Never to sit quietly and brood over adversity, Mario accepted a bid from Ford to go NASCAR raiding again. The occasion was the Firecracker 400 at Daytona run, naturally, on the Fourth of July. Ford had also brought in A. J. Foyt. USACer Jim Hurtubise was dealt a Mercury.

Hotshot Charlie Glotzbach snatched the pole, while Foyt could not do better than sixth time. Mario was back in fourteenth place. But NASCAR

In the last fifty laps of the Hanford 250 Mario, Bobby Unser and A. J. Foyt staged one of the hardest fought battles ever with the lead changing constantly. The final finishing order was Foyt, Unser and Andretti—the exact opposite order shown in this picture.

The hundred-miler on the dirt track at DuQuoin in 1968 was the scene
of another Andretti-Foyt battle, as Mario (who started sixth) led A. J.
(who started third) most of the way to the checkered flag.

In his Grand Prix debut (U.S. GP at Watkins Glen) he won the pole position and was the first off the grid. Here he is seen leading the entire field.

racing history shows that no matter where Andretti starts, he'll be up in there if fates and the car stay put.

Well, Mario tried everything, but this was not to be his day either, as Cale Yarborough won and poor Mario, the hex still staring hard on his fortunes, was only able to place twelfth.

Back on the Championship Trail at Castle Rock, Colorado, Foyt pulled into the winner's circle on this hot dusty road course. Mario was able to complete only thirty-five laps, but Bobby Unser finished forty-four laps before he went out.

At Nazareth, on Mario's home grounds, Al Unser nosed out Mario for the flag, and Bobby Unser was seventh.

In the pair of 100-milers at Indianapolis Raceway Park, it was Al Unser's turn again. He was not to be headed, winning both heats. But Mario grimly hung on, taking both second spots, while Bobby Unser took a third and a twenty-first placing, which gave Andretti some more points.

Back at Langhorne for two 100-milers, Mario broke Gordon Johncock's lap record during practice before having a rod snap, preventing him from starting the race. Al Unser took both events.

It had been a long dry spell for the Nazareth flash. Victory lane had given Mario the cold shoulder since Phoenix.

But things looked up at St. Jovite. This was a twin 100-miler and, with any luck, he might score. Mario had run very well up there, having won both 100-mile events the previous year.

With a superb display of skill, Andretti earned the pole position and when he got the flag, there was a crowd pleasing interplay between Mario and Al Unser. Bobby's younger brother was going great guns, having won five races, the best showing of his career. Al managed to gain the upper hand in the four-wheel-drive Lola with Mario pushing for all he was worth. Luck was in Andretti's corner for a change when Al abruptly ran out of fuel with only three laps to go, giving Mario the checkered flag.

But the second go was something else. Mario stormed out in front of Bobby Unser and led the elder of the Unsers by almost three seconds after the first lap. By the time the flag had fallen, Andretti had built up a 46-second lead over the eventual second place finisher, John Cannon.

After picking up his check and 400 points, Mario admitted candidly, "You've got to be lucky to win two races on this track. Naturally, it was a big break when Al ran out of fuel. When the track got oily, that four-wheel-drive was rough to contend with. When the track got dry for the second race, I could really motor."

The Championship crowd went on to DuQuoin for the dirt track 100-miler. Mario nosed out A. J. Foyt in another classic finish to pick up a further sorely needed 200 points. Fortunately for the Nazareth speedster Bobby Unser lasted but five laps.

Having won the Hoosier Hundred the prior two years (1966, 1967) Mario finished second to Foyt (1). Behind them: Roger McCluskey (8) and George Snider (90).

Then came the richest dirt track contest on the USAC trail, the always dramatically competitive Hoosier 100, which in recent years has become a personal combat arena for Foyt and Andretti. Mario took this gem of a race in '66 and '67, but this time it was A. J. who edged out Mario after a furious dice to the flag. Once again Mario got a break in his uphill fight for points with Unser, as Bobby wound up sixteenth.

Taking a brief break from the Championship Trail, Mario and Bobby Unser decided to run a Formula 1 race at Monza, Italy. Andretti was set with Lotus and Unser was making his debut as a Grand Prix driver with BRM.

Through a silly, comic opera antic by the Italian racing officials both USAC stars were barred from running the GP, as they had violated a rule—rarely observed by Monza—of having raced within twenty-four hours of the Monza go, that being the Hoosier race. It was only a 100-miler, but still no dice. Both Mario and Bobby had qualified at Monza and some frantic flying was worked out to get them back and forth.

Needless to say, the Italian racing fans were furious. They wanted to see this great Italian-born racing champion. And naturally Mario wanted to make his Formula 1 debut at the track where, as a boy, he had seen Alberto Ascari.

Then Bobby and Mario renewed their rivalry for the '68 title as they shifted to Trenton. Now the horns of negativism seemed to have locked in on Bobby as he had not once placed well, let alone won, since the "500" in May.

Having been plagued with assorted problems using the turbo Ford engine, Mario startled racing insiders by switching to an Offy for this race—and it paid off. Mario walked away from the field and snatched the checker. Unser could not run his own car, so he drove Mike Mosley's, but could not seem to make it go. Bobby pulled into the pits and got out after eighty-five laps.

Now the point gap was narrowing. The score: Unser 3301; Andretti 3138.

Mario enjoyed the Offy drive: "In a Ford, the power is smooth and constant. But with the Offy, when the turbocharger comes on, it really belts you in the back of your pants. I had to learn to drive the corners all over again. But I'm still a Ford man. When their engine is ready, I'll be using one."

The Sacramento dirt track clambake was another surprise to both Bobby and Mario. Though Andretti had the pole and Unser was sidelined, having racked up in practice, Foyt's good luck and dirt tracking skill brought him the flag after having total mastery of the field. Mario did end up fourth after some tire changes.

Mario has only one area of racing to conquer, winning a Formula 1 race. He had been robbed of his chance at Monza, so he got in a Lotus once more where it counted most—the U. S. Grand Prix at Watkins Glen. During the final ten minutes of qualifying, the dramatic announcement was made that Mario Andretti had snatched the pole position away from a surprised Jackie

Stewart and Mario's teammate, Graham Hill, who virtually "owned" the Glen. It was a big moment.

As for the race? Mario could not finish after battling Stewart for the lead. His clutch gave out. But he had shown his potential. And Colin Chapman was very high on Andretti.

Next was a first-time appearance for the Championship crowd at the exceptionally fast Michigan International Speedway. A dark horse came through a mass of confusion to take this one, Ronnie Bucknum. Poor Mike Mosley got shot down due to the fervent battle for the Championship title. Bobby Unser had been wailing, leading the field and clocking a 178-mph lap when suddenly he blew on the 75th lap. He then jumped into Mosley's car.

Once more Mario was bitten by the fuel bug. With the race bagged, he was forced to gas up six miles from the flag. But his second place finish put him out in front of Bobby by 132 points.

Then came a very critical 250-miler at Hanford. It turned out to be an Unser-Andretti battle, but not for first, as Foyt was able to hang on and take the flag. Foyt, Andretti and Unser mixed it up for the lead off and on. But when it came down to the wire, Mario just could not extract enough power to get by the flat-out Foyt. Bobby got by Mario for second, Mario was third. The point gap was *really* thin! Andretti 3888; Unser 3806.

By some strange quirks of racing, the critical Phoenix 200 was a nightmare for Foyt and Andretti, not to mention Bobby Unser.

Early in the race Foyt and Andretti were locked up in a fiery wreck. Foyt crashed after spinning in some oil. Mario, trying to stay clear, had nowhere to go and bashed Foyt's car. Both broke into flames. A. J. was burned, though not badly, while Mario got slight burns. He would not quit.

Now it was his turn to go car hopping. He dropped into Snider's car. He went from tenth place to fourth in slightly over fifty laps. He moved, but Snider's car was no Hawk. Bobby Unser, also in trouble, again grabbed Mosley's machine but he didn't finish.

It was really a mixed-up affair, as Gary Bettenhausen won his first big car race.

Now came the moment of truth, resulting in the wildest finale of any USAC title battle in its entire history. The stage was Riverside. It was the do-or-die Rex Mays 300. Once again Mario found himself fighting on the same elusive battleground which had cost him the title the previous year.

Mario had a 308 point bulge going in. He didn't have to win. In fact, even if Bobby won, all Mario had to do was finish fifth! The pressure on both Mario and Bobby was fantastic. Goodyear and Firestone were quite up tight too.

To no one's particular surprise, Gurney again sat on the pole, but Mario didn't sandbag to play it safe. He locked up the second fastest time. Bobby

Unser, intent on his first USAC title, didn't overcook. He settled for ninth quickest time.

Gurney was the eventual winner, after staving off a strong bid by Mark Donohue. The thing that *really* grabbed the crowd was the all-out, last ditch stand by Andretti to get the title. He would drive *three* cars before this frantic day was over, to no avail.

It looked so simple. Just hang with Unser, in front—naturally—or just behind. That's all there was to it. But Mario, being the fierce total competitor that he is, refused to cool it or sandbag. He went all out after Gurney. He wanted to win!

After dicing with Dan, and holding the lead for four laps, Mario's engine failed after fifty-nine laps. As luck would again turn on him 'for the second time, his backup car, this time with Jerry Titus up, had fallen out with a broken suspension.

You would not believe what happened next!

After crawling out of his dead car, there was a hurried conversation with Firestone's people and Parnelli Jones, who had acquired a Lotus Turbocar from Andy Granatelli. His driver was Joe Leonard. Joe had been driving a steady race with this brake-weary car on a rough road course.

In came Leonard to the pits. Out he jumped and little Mario leaped in. Now this was something else! Here was a car he had never raced. He had had a few casual laps at Indy with the very tricky Turbocar but not at Riverside. In addition the car had been fitted to six-foot-plus Leonard. The crew frantically stuffed a pillow behind Mario so that he could reach the pedals. Out he went to find Bobby Unser, who had been carefully motoring around. Seeing Andretti's misfortune all Bobby wanted to do was stay in the top ten and what was more important, stay out of trouble. He would have it made.

After a cautious lap to get familiar with the strange machine, Mario elected to get on it. Then by the damndest coincidence in the whacky race this turned out to be, Mario moved alongside fellow Turbocar driver Art Pollard going into the always rough turn nine. He sideslipped and to the shock of all the spectators in view, both Turbocars were immobilized in a brief flash!

Well, one would think after this storybook debacle, Mario would quietly seek a dark corner and get stoned. But more drama was in store.

On a motorscooter came Parnelli. The yellow was out, while Andy Granatelli stood there shocked beyond words, as both of his much argued cars were wiped out on their final appearance—yes they would be illegal next year. As the debris was being cleaned up, Mario piggybacked on the scooter back to the pits.

NOW WHAT?

Gurney's march to victory was virtually ignored by those within view of the Gilbert and Sullivan operetta scene. After some seven laps of earnest con-

Al Unser (5) and Andretti (2), having finished first and second in the first heat of the Indy 200, lead the field for the second hundred-miler.

versation, Lloyd Ruby got the shock of *his* career as he was called in for an unscheduled pit stop. Why? His was the only well-placed Firestone-shod car which could offer any help to the virtually shattered hopes of Andretti salvaging the last ditch stand for the prestige-filled USAC National Championship. It was now lap 70 and a slightly confused and not-too-happy Ruby climbed out and Mario jumped in for his third and final go at Unser.

Well, to end the tension, when this Chinese fire drill ended, Mario finished third behind winner Gurney and Bobby Unser. *But*, having been forced to split his third place points with Lloyd Ruby, it cost him the Championship. Mario Andretti had lost to Bobby Unser by the narrowest margin in National Championship history—*eleven points*!

What could anyone say? After the race, during the press interview, a dead-tired, vastly disappointed Andretti had the courtesy and sportsmanship to join Bobby Unser for the usual battering ram of questions from the press.

Even in the worst defeat he had ever suffered, little Mario Andretti was really a giant that miserable day. He was not bitter. For even though he had fought Unser tooth and tire down to the final race, they were actually very good personal friends. This is the stuff of which *real* champions are made.

Those strange, wispy fates which control the destinies of men who race cars, perhaps, made a quiet note of this modest-sized young man from Nazareth, Pennsylvania. He would have better things in store.

And it would come to pass.

This Was the Year That Was

Despite the disappointment of having been knocked out of the box for the USAC Championship two years in a row at Riverside, Mario Andretti had already racked up a very impressive record.

In four years of full Championship racing he had won two back-to-back titles and had been number two in 1967 and 1968. No matter how you cut it, this young man had stacked up a record few could come near duplicating.

So for 1969 Mario, after having paid a visit to Colin Chapman's Lotus factory in England, planned to buy Colin's drastically new four-wheel-drive car. It would be Ford-powered, for obvious reasons; one, the turbine engine had been so drastically aborted by USAC, it would be less competitive than it had been in '68; two, Mario was a Ford man. The bugs had been worked out of the turbo Ford and it should now come up to expectations. Said Mario: "We should get the new car in time for this year's Five Hundred."

However, two Hawks were being rebuilt for pre-Indy action and as backup cars, just in case. This would later prove to be the best crystal ball thinking the Andretti team had ever done.

As for his racing plans, Mario hoped to run two or three Grand Prix races plus some sports car activity for Ferrari, possibly Daytona's 24 Hours and the Sebring 12 Hours.

Early in March, Mario, along with A. J. Foyt and other top USAC drivers, decided to run the rich $60,000 midget spectacular staged inside the fabulous Houston Astrodome. Mario had long since given up the midget ranks, but the lure of the purse and the unusual rain-proof track was too exciting to miss. The specially built clay track constructed for this single event cost the promoters $50,000 alone!

His first win of the 1969 season was at Hanford where he led from start to finish. Behind him in this photo is teammate Art Pollard.

Bobby Unser (1) and Mario swapped the lead several times at Langhorne before a deflating tire slowed Andretti and put him out of contention.

His victory in the Trenton 200 marked his twenty-sixth Championship
victory. Wally Dallenbach (22) led for more than half the race,
but his Offy was no match for Andretti's Ford on the straights.

Mario, Bobby and Al Unser formed a special "partnership" for this one-of-a-kind race. They elected to pool their Astro winnings—if lucky—and divide the total money equally.

As Mario puts it: "We decided to put everything into one pot. During Saturday's race—it was a two-day affair—I didn't feel too bad as Bobby was near the front and Al in the middle. I was way back and figured all I would try to do was finish. It worked out pretty good the first day. Al and Bobby did finish well up in the money."

As for the second race on Sunday, the situation was not quite as rosy. Says Mario, "During Sunday's go, again I thought I could relax and let them carry the load. Bobby and Al were running up near the front and running well. Then all of a sudden I looked over and saw Bobby standing by his car in the infield and I thought, 'So what? Al's still running good.' The next thing I knew, both of them were standing in the infield and waving me on.

"So I figured I had to carry the load for all three of us and started to go faster. I promptly lost three places." Mario sighs and then smiles slightly. In fact, none of the USAC big-time artillery fared well.

Early in March, Mario flew to South Africa for another whack at running a team Formula 1 Lotus. He put on a fine show, dicing with Jackie Stewart, until his transmission failed.

Mario had this to say about that venture:

"My Lotus was a little older than Rindt's or Hill's, but as far as the vital components were concerned, I had as fair a shake as they did. I did have a smaller transmission. As hard as you have to run in Formula One today, I certainly couldn't pussyfoot around and hope to be competitive. So I did run hard and perhaps it was too much for that gearbox. As far as running with a wing or airfoil, the size makes a great deal of difference. You can take some parts of a race course flat out which would be impossible without a wing. But when I broke my regular wing, they replaced it with a smaller one and, man, it was like running an entirely different race car."

He added he hoped to run as many GPs as his crowded schedule would permit. And of course, Mario would be going after the now elusive USAC title again.

It was down to Sebring for the tough twelve-hour grind to co-drive a prototype three-liter Ferrari with Chris Amon. It was the sole factory entry, taking on a massive array of the new big-engined Porsches. John Wyer of England brought over his now "antique" GT40 Fords. With factory Ford and Chaparral out of competition, it was expected the Porsches would run away with the flag. But it wound up being one of the most exciting, suspense-filled events

Three-wheeling it and kicking up the dirt on his way
to winning the Tony Bettenhausen 100 at DuQuoin.

Driving his backup car, the STP Hawk, he's on his way to winning the Indy "500."

◀ Mario and Andy undergo questions from reporters during
a press conference following their first Indianapolis "500" victory.

About to lap Roger McCluskey en route to victory in the elusive Rex Mays 300.

STP teammates Andretti and Pollard did not fare well at the
season-opener at Phoenix. Both were sidelined with mechanical problems.

Co-driving a prototype, three-liter Ferrari with Chris Amon
at the 12 Hours of Sebring, they managed to finish second.

ever seen in Sebring's history. As expected, the fleet Porsches hopped into the lead, with Chris Amon pushing hard. The lead German cars had to really motor to stave off the bird dogging Ferrari, which had taken the pole away from the chagrined Porsche army.

After about three hours of hard racing, the pressures exerted by Andretti and Amon began to extract their Porsche toll. The lead Porsche spent eleven minutes in the pits for suspension reworking. After the sixth hour another factory Porsche went out with a cracked chassis. In the seventh hour another lead Porsche gave way to the screaming V12 Ferrari. Then still another Porsche collapsed.

Suddenly Amon had to dodge a spinning smaller car. In doing so he bent up the cooling vents for the engine and later steamed into the pits because of overheating.

In the ninth hour Andretti was black flagged, as the side lights, which lit up the car number, had failed. After another weird Ferrari pit stop, a flashlight was substituted, taped to the door!

Then, in another pit stop to halt the overheating, a burst of flame poured out of the Ferrari's engine room. It was put out, but now the car had to run at low rpm in order to save the engine and to finish.

Being forced to run at a reduced speed, a lone GT40 Ford, which had slowly worked its way up, got by the frustrated Amon and Andretti to take the checkered flag at 10:00 P.M. So Mario finished second, but on the way he and Amon had literally driven the Porsche team cars into the ground.

Three days later in New York a special press luncheon was held by the always unpredictable Andy Granatelli. He had two announcements. One was not very unusual; that he was buying four new Lotus Indy cars from Colin Chapman. However, the second was a bombshell. He had signed Mario Andretti to drive the '69 season for STP!

It seemed that Mario's sponsorship with Overseas National Airways had ended and, from what could be gleaned from the bits and pieces of conversation, Mario wanted to concentrate on driving and not be saddled with the worries of being a car owner.

It was a wild pairing; the most famous Italian-Americans in racing were tied together. When called upon, Mario had a few funny comments: "With the bad luck we've both had at Indy, plus Andy's twenty-year search for a victory, maybe we can both end this jinx." Mario made it clear that his team would remain intact and that Brawner and McGee would run his operation as usual.

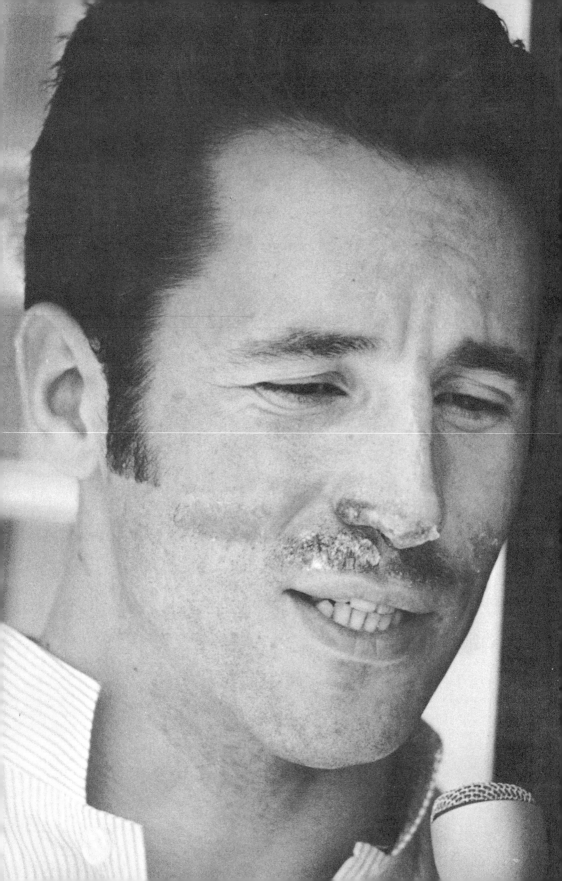

The fastest car at the Speedway in 1969 was utterly demolished when a
wheel came off in the number four turn while Mario was running at about
150 mph. The STP Lotus slammed into the wall and burst into flames
as it spun on down the track. Mario was extremely lucky to have escaped
with nothing more serious than facial burns.

Mario's first appearance with his Hawk painted the screaming bright red of STP was at the season USAC opener at Phoenix. The race turned into a mechanical demolition derby. One by one, all the top leaders fell out for some reason or another; Bobby Unser, Al Unser, A. J. Foyt, Roger McCluskey and finally, Mario. He was sidelined with a broken half shaft. Was his jinx starting again? He recalled that not only had Andy Granatelli never won Indy, but his cars had never even won a single Championship race!

Meanwhile reports from England indicated that early tests of the STP Lotus cars were exceptionally good. They could really move. On April 8 Mario tested the first new Lotus 64 Indy car at Hanford. It was very quick and showed it had what Andretti wanted.

At long last, Granatelli's dry racing spell was ended when Mario captured the Hanford 200-miler. He was on the pole and led from start to finish. He was now third in points.

The Trenton 200, which always had preceded the trip to Indianapolis had to be postponed, as the new, extended, mile-and-a-half track was not ready. The surface was too bumpy.

Mario was eagerly looking forward to Indianapolis practice and qualifications. For one thing, the turbo Ford engine was really running now. Various alterations had been made, and at practice sessions at Indy in April and early May they were outrunning the turbo Offy. Mario was quite excited about his new Lotus. It handled beautifully and in the corners its four-wheel-drive produced extraordinary control.

On May 12 Mario posted his fastest time ever at the Brickyard: a lap of 170.179. The next day he went out to "burn in" a new set of brakes and promptly upped his time to 171.494.

The rains came again and, for the first time in the memory of Indianapolis, the first weekend of qualifying was washed out. Some 150,000 hardy souls had come to see the hoped-for qualifying battle between Andretti, Foyt and Roger McCluskey. The only ones pleased by the rainout were Graham Hill and Denis Hulme. They were able to fly out early for the Monaco GP.

During practice earlier that week, Foyt had joined Mario in the rarefied atmosphere of the "over 170 mph" club. Then Mario turned in four laps all of which were over 171, with a peak lap of 171.567.

The following day, Mario pumped his mark up again, extracting 171.798. Foyt, as usual, was right on his tail pipes, cutting a 170.908 lap.

The final week of practice, which followed the qualifying rainout, brought Mario one of the most terrifying disasters of his entire racing career. He had

Aldo and members of the STP and Firestone crews run down
the pits to get in on the Victory Lane celebration.

the Lotus out for some fresh tuneup runs. He stood on the throttle going down the back stretch and was wailing through the fourth turn when all hell broke loose.

As Mario tells it: "I heard the engine zing, which meant it was overrevving. I knew something had happened. It was the right rear wheel coming off. There was not a thing I could do. I knew I was going to hit the wall and would clobber it pretty hard, and I did."

By his own admission, Mario was the luckiest man in the world at that moment. He had totally destroyed the Lotus, tearing everything off the "tub," or basic chassis shell. Then the car caught fire.

"I started unstrapping myself right away and trying to get out. The fire may not have looked like much right then, but it was burning pretty good. I was out just moments after the car stopped," says Mario.

Teammate Art Pollard, in the STP Plymouth-powered wedge car had his share of shock, for he was about 200 feet behind Mario when the rear hub broke. As he tells it:

"I had never followed Mario around the track before. When he came out, I thought I'd fall in and follow him. I guess we were doing around 150 through the fourth turn. Suddenly I saw the wheel come off Mario's car. The wheel hit the wall first, a good hundred feet before his car did. Then other parts began flying.

"When he hit the wall, pieces were flying all over the place. He just had to sit there and wait for the car to stop. I cut down the track, trying to stay away from the wreckage. I began dodging pieces from the Lotus and then the entire rear of his car came sliding down in front of me. I cut back up the track and locked my brakes.

"I slid through some of the fire and finally stopped about fifty feet short of the wreckage, as Mario was climbing out. I ran over to him and he seemed okay except for burns on his upper lip.

"I've never seen a car break up like that. It looked as though four or five cars had been involved because there was so much wreckage flying around—the nose cone, chunks of the body, the entire rear section and the transmission. He's mighty lucky to get out of that one and so was I."

This was the understatement of the year, or any year, as far as Mario Andretti was concerned.

Now a pall of gloom had settled on the STP team. The best chance of taking the pole and winning had been wiped out. Then came another crusher. Because of the structural weakness in the wheel hubs it was decided to withdraw the other two Lotus cars of Jochen Rindt and Graham Hill. There was not enough time to fabricate new parts. Now two of the most talented drivers from Europe were out of action, having not even been able to try to qualify.

As for Mario, he had but one avenue open. That would be to run his 1968

Hawk. By this bit of fortune, through the efforts of Clint Brawner, he would at least have a car to run—the best running Lotus now being a basket case.

The Granatelli jinx was still riding herd on this man. There are some who don't like Andy, but even the most hard nosed of these could not keep from agreeing that he had gotten more than his share of lumps.

So with the tenacity for not quitting which has always been a key factor in Mario Andretti's success pattern, he brought his familiar white Hawk, now repainted STP red, and went about the business of qualifying.

When the job was done, A. J. Foyt, seeking his fourth "500" victory was on the pole with a 170.568. A malfunctioning turbocharger waste gate had foiled his bid to crack Joe Leonard's 1968 mark. The Hawk ran well and Andretti was able to lock up second position with a 169.851.

Now it was time to race. At least Mario had this going for him—he knew the Hawk was reliable, race proven. The engine was strong. There might be a problem with fuel consumption, for the powerful Fords were using up more fuel than the Offies. Brawner was somewhat pessimistic about going the entire 500 miles with the limited fuel tank size.

Last year's winner, Bobby Unser, had been up to his ears in difficulty with his new four-wheel-drive Lola. The drive units appeared out of whack. But Mark Donohue, here for the first time, had no trouble with the same kind of car.

The field was on the grid. Mario sat in his car thinking, as he waited for Tony Hulman's time-honored command "Gentlemen, start your engines!" Would this be his third straight collapse here? He could win everything but this damned race, the most important event in the world.

The thirty-three cars moved out. Then came the tension packed moment. The cars were moaning down through the fourth turn, with Mario flanked by Foyt and Bobby Unser. The green flag came down, and a giant roar of screaming engines, plus a thunderous ovation from the hundred thousand fans lining the main straight, filled the bright Indiana sky which was dotted with colorful balloons.

Into the first turn it was Mario. He recalls: "I hadn't consciously thought about taking the lead at the start. But I got on the pedal from force of habit. I wasn't going to give that first turn to Foyt. If he had beat me in, I'd have had to back off. Instead I did get there first and took advantage of it."

So for the first five laps it was Andretti, Foyt and McCluskey. Roger, in Foyt's team car, was running very well. But on the sixth tour of this historic track, Foyt flashed by Andretti. Shortly after that McCluskey slipped by into second place. Why?

Mario explains: "I found out I could run with anybody out there. But at this fast pace, my water temperature began to soar. Water began spewing back into the cockpit and I had to back off and drive by the gauges. I found

Opening up a big lead over Denis Hulme in the Texas Can-Am, Andretti
became the first man to have beaten the McLarens, even if only for a little while.

Most USAC drivers stay away from Pikes Peak, feeling that it's Unser territory, but Mario entered "the race to the clouds"—and won.

The people of Mario's hometown of Nazareth, Pennsylvania, staged a Mario Andretti Day parade, complete with floats, and renamed the street where he lives Victory Lane.

◀ After hitting the inside rail on lap 88 of the Hoosier Hundred, Mario continued on with a broken wheel and a deflated tire to complete the 100 laps and finish sixth behind teammate Greg Weld who was the fastest qualifier.

out just how fast I could run without having any trouble and I stuck to that range pretty good."

It should be mentioned here that less than fourteen hours before the race Mario was not sure his engine would last even one-quarter of the race. He knew overheating would be a factor, so Brawner had installed an extra radiator after qualifying. It was spotted by several people, including Foyt. A protest was lodged. The radiator had to come off.

Mario followed this restrained pattern in the race. It must have been difficult, as the front runners switched around. When Foyt pitted for fuel on lap 52, Wally Dallenbach had his brief moment of glory by taking the lead until he had to pit. Foyt quickly regained the front position. Then Mr. Hard Luck of Indianapolis, Lloyd Ruby, came charging up. He had started twentieth and moved up to sixth place in ten laps. He began riding shotgun on his fellow Texan. Then Foyt's supercharger began acting up.

On lap 79 Ruby whipped by and took over. Mario found himself moved up to the point where he could move in, and did. He assumed the lead on lap 87.

Foyt was not destined to win this year. The waste gate problem that plagued him during qualifying returned. This malfunction cost him twenty-three laps in the pits and put him beyond any possible contention.

Ruby, realizing that Mario was forced to hold down his engine rpm, turned on the juice and took command again on lap 103. But three laps later Mario pushed his throttle hard enough to get by Ruby again. Then Ruby was victimized in the pits by an errant crewman who signaled him to blast off onto the track. Unfortunately one fuel hose was still locked to the car's tank. Result: a torn tank that dropped him out for good.

"As much as I later felt sorry for him," says Mario, "I was relieved when old Rube dropped out. He was the guy who was really worrying me. I knew I could run with Foyt and McCluskey but every time I eased off a bit to let my gauges get back to normal, I'd look in the mirror and there was Ruby again. He was determined to win this thing. Believe me, I knew how he felt. So when he went out, I decided to drive carefully and stay out of trouble."

Contender Roger McCluskey burned out his exhaust header and Dallenbach had snapped his clutch. Joe Leonard was black flagged after 127 laps, but he went out again to eventually wind up sixth.

Now the only challenger left for Mario to be concerned with was Dan Gurney, formidable under any normal circumstances. He had finished second the previous year and naturally was hungry for the biggest checkered flag of all. But as he began to move in on Mario, his stock block engine began making strange noises, and Mario's crew gave out the sign, "Gurney sour."

Then came the "EZ" sign. Mario did just that.

"When I knew I had the lead by a good margin, I backed way off," he says.

While Al Unser was leading the Trenton 300, Bobby Unser (1), Mario (2) and A. J. Foyt (6) waged a nerve-tingling, three-way battle for second place. When the checkered flag fell, however, it was Andretti who had gotten there first. Points earned in this race boosted his lead to such a great margin that no other driver stood a chance of winning the Championship. After losing the Championship by a small margin for the past two years, Andretti clinched the title with several races still to be run. Secure in the knowledge that the coveted #1 was theirs, Mario and co-chief mechanics Clint Brawner and Jim McGee were a very happy trio in Victory Circle.

"And I kept going slower. Those last forty laps or so, I was way down in the one-fifties and when it got down to the last ten laps, I was praying and driving as carefully as I could. I didn't want anything to happen to the engine now. I kept a sharp eye way ahead so I could spot any trouble.

"I had planned to take it easy until the last thirty laps. Then if I was still in contention, I'd give the engine everything it would take. But I never had to make that move. When the checkered flag was waved, I almost couldn't believe it!"

You may safely bet your final farthing that the biggest disbeliever at the whole track was one Andy Granatelli. It was the greatest all-Italian victory since the Romans divided Gaul into three parts. In Victory Lane a wildly emotional Granatelli bussed Mario soundly on the cheek.

"When I crashed the Lotus, I thought it was all over," Mario reflects. "Maybe the way it turned out was the best thing that could have happened, as the Lotus might not have gone the distance. But when I got into the Hawk, it was just like being back home. This car is my baby."

Even the usually blasé chief steward, Harlan Fengler, says: "Andretti was the most popular winner of them all."

Flushed with success, Mario turned to the next business at hand: his bid to regain the National Championship.

At Milwaukee it appeared this race would be in the bag. Mario won the pole. He opened up a four-second lead after twelve laps, but a bugged magneto cut down his speed. Then he ran out of fuel. At least teammate Art Pollard salvaged a victory for STP—and a first Championship win for himself.

Mario had hopes of running for Lotus in the Formula I Grand Prix in Holland, but the rained-out Langhorne race washed out those plans at the same time. At Langhorne he broke the one-mile record in a standard, unsupercharged Ford engine. Commenting about what appeared to be an unusual move, Mario points out: "I wanted better gas mileage. You don't need that kind of supercharged power here. It's that kind of track." When the race was finally run a week later, Bobby Unser broke his long losing streak by winning. He had not won a race since the 1968 Indy "500"! Mario had driven a great race with a slowly deflating tire. He knew that if he pitted, that would be the race. It was a masterful bit of controlled driving. He did end up fifth.

On June 29 Mario added another remarkable facet to his varied winning career. He ran the tricky, fantastic Pike's Peak hillclimb and won the Championship class. This windy, dangerous 12½-mile mountain has been an Unser province for forty years. Many USAC drivers won't take it on, as they feel there's little hope with the Unsers around. But Mario did and again demonstrated his amazing skills at a highly specialized form of racing. After Mario had won, Andy Granatelli, who was about fifteen miles down at the start line, made kissing sounds over the radio communications system to

Mario who asked Andy why he didn't say anything.

"I'm giving you a kiss, you dope," answered Granatelli. "Great," said Mario from up top, "but I'm eating a ham sandwich and that's better than one of your kisses!"

At Continental Divide Raceway, the Championship cars took on another road race. Andretti drove well there, but he suffered a bad oil leak, which dropped him out of competition.

There was time out for a well-deserved "Mario Andretti Day" in his home-town of Nazareth. The obviously proud little town of some 10,000 souls staged a two-hour parade in his honor. That night he went to the track and bagged the 100-mile Championship dirt track affair. (How *could* he lose this one?) After the race, he rushed to the hospital where at about two the next morning, his wife presented him with a baby girl. And that was a day for him to remember.

There had been a party at Mario's house that afternoon after the parade. With a broad grin Mario commented: "Many people here in town thought I'd never amount to anything. Maybe they are right. Here I am at twenty-nine and I don't have a steady job."

The Nazareth win marked the twenty-fifth Championship victory of his marvelous career. He was now second only to Foyt in all-time Championship flags.

At Trenton, after whacking the wall in practice, which called for a new wheel, Mario took the pole and the race away in the final stages from a hard-charging Wally Dallenbach. Making an early unscheduled pit stop, he fueled up and ran hard while the others eventually had to come in. But at the end Andretti was practically running on fumes, his fuel was that low.

At Indianapolis Raceway Park another one of those human lapses cost Mario this road race. After charging with Dan Gurney, Mario was forced to pit with a loose rear wheel. A long pit stop set him far back and he could only finish ninth. However, Mario still had over a 1000-point lead in his quest for the title, as he was being helped by wins scored by what you might call unexpected drivers, not his major contenders. Peter Revson won at IRP, for example—it was his first on the Trail.

Back at Milwaukee, it was Al Unser's day in the sun. Mario had qualified next to Unser on the front row. But again this was to be a day of strange con-fusion which often plagues drivers; good and also rans. About midway, he rolled in to refuel but did not get a full load, and his car ran dry again near the end. He took a fourth.

The very next day there was a dirt track go at Springfield. Though Greg Weld sat on the pole, it was Mario who went East with the money and the flag. It was clear now that Andretti had honed to a fine point his dirt track driving technique. He snatched the lead and never let it go.

He managed to squeeze in enough time to test a Can-Am car with a Ford engine worked up by Holman and Moody. He seemed well pleased with the big bore 494ci power plant. For the first time he had power to play with and planned some Can-Am excursions before the season ended.

The big cars went to a totally new track at Dover Downs in Delaware. It's a high banked affair which was ideal for stockers, but tough on the light Championship cars. Accidents which took out Dallenbach, Al Unser and Mario marred the race. Brawner was very unhappy with the place, and Mario didn't care much for it either. Few of the USACers wanted to go back.

Again it was Al Unser's turn to win at DuQuoin. Now he was threatening brother Bobby for second place in the point standings, while Mario maintained his strong number one edge.

That same weekend Mario flew to Elkhart Lake to run the big-engined McLaren Ford. The car was a year old, which was somewhat of a handicap. Handling was a problem, but Mario seemed unconcerned: "All I want is an engine. They will build a car to go around it."

He did qualify third behind the tough Kiwis, Denis Hulme and Bruce McLaren. But in the prerace practice session, a suspension upright tore loose, while braking for a turn. After some frantic pit work, Mario stormed out just in time to join the pace lap, but to no avail. A rear U joint had been destroyed. No race that day.

Now it was time for the yearly Foyt-Andretti "exhibition" at the Hoosier 100, which was televised live to the nation. It was A. J.'s turn this time after taking over half the race to catch the front runners. Mario had led the first fifty-five miles but began to have trouble with the very hard track surface. His suspension setting, evidently quite stiff, shredded a tire and finally a wheel rim cracked. He wound up sixth.

Then it was still another road race, this time at Brainerd, Minnesota— Donnybrooke raceway, twisting foreign land to most of the Championship drivers. Mario appeared to lose power in the first 100-mile heat. He couldn't really get going, but finished fourth. By taking third in the second heat, Mario picked up another 260 points.

The Trenton 300 was the most important race of the year for Mario. He hauled in his twenty-eighth big car win and locked up his third National Championship. He started sixth with a totally new Hawk. Trying a new fuel injection system for better mileage proved a little costly in horsepower. But Mario drove a heads-up race. Unable to take Bobby Unser's hot Offy, Mario waited. Then he took over on the 142nd lap. By lap 185 he had stacked up an overwhelming six-lap lead. Then a tire began losing air, but he nursed it into Victory Lane.

"It's a relief knowing I won't have to sweat things out for the next few

Not even Mario's considerable talents could turn this non-competitive
four-wheel-drive Lotus into a winner at Watkins Glen.

months," said a very happy winner, "and now I can go to Riverside and really race. Gurney's going to have to work a lot harder this time!"

At Sacramento on the dirt again, Al Unser pulled this one out of the bag, as Mario failed to finish.

Then Mario went to Watkins Glen for the U.S. Grand Prix. Not only did he thirst for a Formula I victory, but this would be the place to do it. Unfortunately he was stuck with the four-wheel-drive Lotus. No one had been able to make it work; not even Hill or Rindt. Mario struggled with it vainly in practice. Even though the car was a dog, this totally competitive young man took it into the race, knowing that he had virtually no chance of winning. So out he went on race day and stormed off the grid with all four tires smoking. Going up the long hill on the first lap, he appeared to have been tapped on the rear. Three laps later he was out with a broken suspension.

There was sympathy for this gutsy champion. Said one veteran fan: "Being asked to test a car is one thing, but doing it in front of one hundred thousand people is something else, especially after having taken the pole position here last year and his great record this year. It just isn't fair."

Mario then got into his year-old McLaren and went out to do the Can-Am at Monterey in California. In practice he broke the qualifying record of the previous year. In the race the suspension uprights were giving trouble again. After some heavy battling, Andretti came in fourth. It was just a case of getting a strong, competitive car.

At Kent, Washington, in a pair of 100-milers, Mario won the first heat and placed second in the final heat.

Then another quick switch from Championship cars to the Can-Am trail once more, this time at Riverside, a course which Mario knows all too well. When the tough contest was over, Mario came in third behind Chuck Parsons, who was in turn headed by winner Denny Hulme.

Things looked better in the big Ford-engined car as Mario again fought the battle of McLaren and Hulme at the Texas Speedway Can-Am. This time he was on the front of the grid beside Hulme. Going well, he was ousted within ten laps by a blown piston.

Al Unser took the Phoenix Championship race, as Mario and Bobby Unser crashed.

Then came the final race of the 1969 season, the ill-fated—at least for Mario—Rex Mays 300 at Riverside. But now, with the Championship locked up, he could afford to be loose, to go all out without worrying about Foyt or Unser.

As things turned out, Mario staged a thrilling, come-from-behind thirty-seven-second margin of victory. Gurney had led most of the way, then his

Even top USAC Championship stars occasionally try their
hands at the Midgets as did Mario at the inaugural Astro Grand Prix.

Eagle came up with differential failure, which caused him to slow down. Mario closed in and got him.

But it must be noted that Mario had his troubles mechanically. Getting underway, Gurney swung out into the lead. Then Mario got by Mark Donohue to ride herd on the man he wanted to beat. On the seventh lap the bright red Hawk was out in front. Then Gurney repassed. Donohue tried to go by, but had to drop back.

Mario had to pit on the thirteenth lap of this 300-miler for a left rear wheel change. The wing nut was not seated properly.

"I almost crashed in three successive corners before I could get back to the pits for the change," admits Mario.

But that was not the only problem. The balance bar for the brakes went out in the early laps and Andretti thus had no rear brakes.

Says Mario: "I kept locking the front brakes and I just couldn't stay with Gurney or Donohue in the corners."

After the forced pit stop, he was back in tenth place.

Abruptly, Donohue, taking the lead from Gurney, dropped out with a battered gearbox. Mario began working his way up again even with the handicap of no rear brakes. Soon he was in third place.

Mario had to pit again and lost third, for the time being, to Bobby Unser, who was six seconds ahead of him. Mario caught Bobby and repassed him. Twenty laps later, he got by a slowing Gurney and unlapped himself.

Finally he closed the big gap and took Gurney, a victory he had to work for. Had he not had the difficulties outlined and if Gurney had not experienced his, it would have been a tossup as to who would have won. But that's racing.

So Mario Andretti wound up with one of the greatest records in USAC competition. Certainly it was his finest year. He took the Championship by the largest point margin ever recorded in Indianapolis car history—a total of 5025 points. Al Unser, who outpointed brother Bobby, had but 2630.

As for the future?

The talent is unquestionably there, all that remains for more great seasons is the equipment. You may be sure Mario Andretti will do his best to have that equipment and the men needed to set it up.

Mario

What is it that some drivers are given which sets them apart from their fellow practitioners? The usual argument is that some are born with their skills and all they need is opportunity. Then there are those who say that any brave, well-coordinated young man can be trained, or "schooled," and given the right equipment.

Some of the latter is true, but we still feel that a real champion must have certain natural gifts to begin with.

There are many so-called brave drivers who don't know what the word fear means. They are capable of getting into a racing machine and sticking their feet to the floor and can extract the maximum speed available. But this ability rarely produces a top drawer, skilled driver.

In the early days of racing, brute strength, stamina and pure guts were the primary talents needed.

But today's super sophisticated cars demand much more of a top driver. Racing now takes full-time, serious concentration. The first-rank driver has to have a basic knowledge of racing car design and a certain amount of mechanical ability.

So what sets Mario Andretti apart? How does he fit in that rarefied atmosphere reserved for perhaps a handful of super drivers?

One way to evaluate him is to turn to the professionals in and about racing. Praise from such people is not tossed around loosely.

One of USAC's all-time greats, Rodger Ward, has this to say: "Mario has a natural feel for a race car. He seems to have sensitive nerves in the seat of his pants. He can 'feel' the car through a situation. His determination and depth perception are a little greater. He's got an edge on most of the drivers right now. He's got a lot of confidence in addition to everything else."

Another crack Indy car veteran not given to a lot of meaningless conversation is Parnelli Jones. He's impressed with Mario's will to win. "It's the same drive you need in football, golf or even in business. And he has it. You have

Pretty DeeAnn waits for Mario to complete interviews in Victory Circle at Trenton.

A carefree moment between practice sessions finds rivals Parnelli Jones and Mario strolling through the pits apparently joking about how to take a turn.

to be aggressive. A. J. Foyt is probably the most determined, aggressive driver around. But if I had to choose a driver, I'd take Andretti, because he's easier to get along with."

Then there is the vitally important factor of knowing the machinery. Mario has a natural feel for sensing out the performance potential of the car he's involved with.

A man who has been around racing for about thirty years is Chris Economaki, known mainly to most racing fans as a racing commentator for ABC's "Wide World of Sports." Chris has been around virtually every kind of track since he was in his teens.

He recalls seeing Mario during the very early days at the Teaneck Armory in New Jersey running three-quarter midgets. It was Mario's first go in open cockpit cars:

"I thought Andretti had a lot of promise even in those days. When he began to make a name for himself, I had heard that Al Dean was looking for a young driver with promise. Clint Brawner asked me who was good, so I told him about Mario.

"Today Mario is considered the best development driver in the country. To point up his natural sense for the feel of a car, his crew could change a rear sway bar on Mario's car without telling him. Now the difference in thickness and tension of one sway bar when the graduation, or setting is changed, is minuscule. Mario would come in after two laps and say, 'You changed the sway bar.' He has an uncanny feel for things mechanical where other drivers who are as good on the track as he is just don't have that extra sense needed to sort things out on a complex racing car."

Economaki says further, "Mario could become the greatest driver America has ever seen. He has the versatility and the skills and he's still young enough to rack up a great record."

Many officials at both Ford Motor Company and Firestone Tire and Rubber Co. candidly admit Mario is their favorite driver. He rarely displays temper tantrums. He lives up to his agreements. If he says he'll be somewhere for a personal appearance, he's there. On the professional side, a Firestone racing director says: "Mario's wonderful for tire testing because if you ask him to run at 165 mph, he'll go out and run exactly that."

Ford's racing director Jacque Passino calls him "a real pro who knows how to evaluate a car. At Sebring, for example, Mario came up with the fact that the Mark IV was bottoming, although he was running on a virtually flat surface. At Daytona, he suggested some sway bar changes that corrected the Fairlane. And in testing at Kingman, Arizona, he told us the car would run faster without a certain spoiler around the sides and back. And he was right."

Then there are the men who like racing as a sport, but mainly as a business —the track promoters.

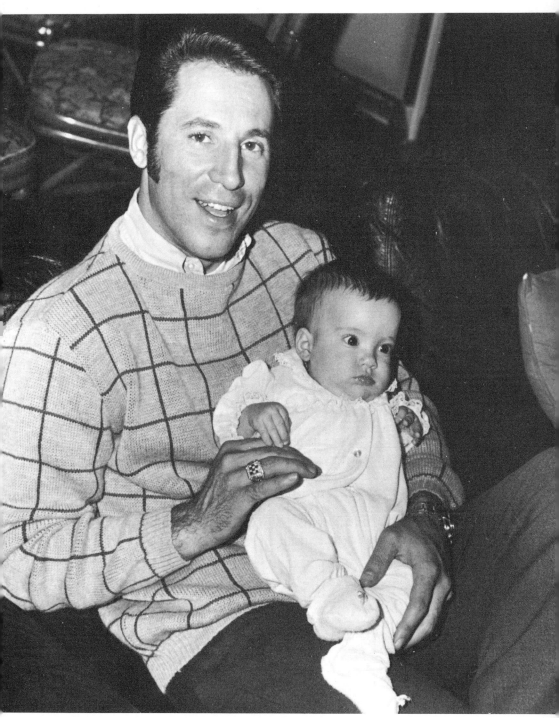

Daughter Barbra Dee was born late at night after the Mario Andretti Day parade and Mario's winning the Nazareth 100—it had been quite a day for the Andrettis.

One such man sums up his impressions of Mario. He's Irving Fried, who has been promoting races since 1941 at Langhorne Speedway in Pennsylvania. This is a tough track to drive. In fact Mario says sometimes it's harder than Indianapolis.

"You've got to concentrate all the time at Langhorne. The setup of the track is such that you can never relax. You're on and off the gas pedal all the way around."

Fried says, "When I first saw him, I figured this little guy was a comer. He looked to be 'all race driver.' The more I saw him race, the more I became convinced that he was going to hang up a tremendous record. In my book, after having seen two generations of racing drivers, he's got to be one of the greatest.

"Also, something that is naturally important to those of us who stage races; Mario is very popular with the fans. He's always very gracious. I wouldn't know how to come up with any adverse criticism. He's a fine guy to deal with. He doesn't have to take a back seat to anybody."

Mario has a combination of various important factors that few of his fellow drivers in USAC share; a burning desire to prove his talents in all fields of racing. He's not satisfied in topping the list in his major racing area of interest, Championship cars, but also he wants to excel in sports cars, stockers and Formula cars. This is especially admirable not only from a broadened, diversified standpoint, but with today's expanded racing schedule, it's remarkable that he finds time to do it.

Parnelli Jones has some thoughts about this. Now Parnelli, after he had achieved what he wanted in racing, after he had driven the world's most advanced racing car at Indianapolis in 1967—the ill-fated STP Turbocar—has eased off his racing schedule. He doesn't want to run Indy cars now, but picks and chooses his rides. He thinks that Mario will come around to this eventually: "One of these days, Mario will burn himself out and ask himself, 'What in hell am I doing here?' "

From the present atmosphere, it's doubtful that will come about with Mario for some time.

"I want to keep driving for ten or twenty years," he says. "I figure I was put on earth to drive race cars."

There are perhaps two men in racing who have similar outlooks: A. J. Foyt and Dan Gurney.

Mario not only has won just about every major race in the various kinds of racing he participates in, but he has earned admiration and respect wherever he has gone.

He has never exhibited the "I am a star" complex which has chilled many people toward certain big-name drivers who shall be nameless here. He listens carefully, exchanges vital information and, like the late Jimmy Clark, when he's ready to race, he's all business.

When he ran at Watkins Glen in the Lotus in 1968 and gained the pole, this was a source of pride to many American racing fans.

Louis Stanley, head of the BRM team, an articulate, intelligent long-time observer of the Grand Prix racing scene, has this to say of Mario: "His handling of the Lotus Ford at the Glen was masterly. If he decides to take part in the World Championship, his talent will be very much on the rise."

Ferrari would, it's said, almost place his factory in hock to get Mario. After all, he's a true Italian and it has been a long dry spell since Ferrari has had a truly great native-born driver. There's little question that with the Ferrari design genius and Mario Andretti as his number one driver, he could recapture the World Championship.

Mario's stellar performance at Sebring and Daytona has proven his natural ability in sports cars. His dogged determination to score in the Canadian-American Challenge Cup series has drawn much acclaim. The races so far have been in cars which were not competitive to the far superior McLarens, but he has run with this handicap because he truly loves to race.

As a person, racing reporters have usually found him receptive, polite and cooperative. He is rarely surly, or insulting.

Instead of living the big, expensive life, Mario still lives in the little Pennsylvania town where he came as a relatively poor boy, where he worked in a gas station before making the big time.

He married his high school sweetheart. They have three delightful children.

Mario's intensive racing involvement makes life somewhat difficult for the personable, pretty young girl to whom Mario is married. But she was well aware of what was in store for her with this restless, star-struck young man.

What DeeAnn Andretti knows, of course, is that she can't have the normal, average, nine-to-five American life and Mario would be the first to admit that his own life is abnormal.

There are strains that DeeAnn manages to solve beautifully. For example, their family spends the whole month of May at Indianapolis. They finally built a large, comfortable split-level home in Nazareth valued at $100,000. But Mario may spend all of sixty days a year in it.

"It's an unreasonable situation, I know it," admits Mario. "If I stay home one weekend, I get irritable. Try to take the kids to the park. There is no way I can do that. On a weekday, okay. But if there's a race in Kalamazoo, I've got to be there."

What makes a man want to drive that much? If you have never known the feeling, the burning rage to race, there is no way to make you understand. Why do supermillionaires like Bob Hope and Jack Benny keep working?

Because they love the business that is show business. Racing is no different.

There is a final commentary of the "why" of Mario Andretti that is best explained by himself:

"You have to be a dedicated person. You have to want to do it more than anything else. You have to want to be Number One. Then you have to have the ability. You must be brave, but also have common sense.

"There's a point where you have to shut off and where you have to be competitive. You must drive not only with your foot, but also your brain."

As for the danger element: "I know that things can happen. As deeply involved as I am in racing I know what can happen and that I have taken chances, but then, I know what I'm doing when I take those chances.

"To be good a driver has to take chances. The guy who has confidence and pushes it to the limit, that is a real race driver."

At thirty, Mario Andretti has a future rarely available to others who ply this dangerous, but tremendously exciting trade.

He knows where he wants to go. He would like, it is thought, to become the greatest, most versatile driver in the history of racing.

He may become just that.

Mario with his sons Michael, seven, and Jeffrey, six,
in front of one of Mario's trophy cases.

These pictures and the ones on the pages that follow show the sequence of events as Mario prepares for a race. (Left) After arriving at the track, Mario hops out of his rented car and starts to don his driver's suit. . . . (Above) As his mechanics prepare his car, he clocks the times the other drivers are turning in. . . .

(Left) He checks the speeds which have already been posted. . . .
(Above) Getting a push from co-chief mechanic Jim McGee (behind
right rear tire) and a crew member, he goes out to practice. . . .

Not completely satisfied with the running of the car, he comes back into the pits to have co-chief mechanic Clint Brawner make some adjustments. . . .

Having qualified, he watches his competition and thinks about how he's going to run the race. . . .

◀ With qualifying completed and the race about to begin, Mario gets ready to go.

A total competitor, Andretti is willing to try any form of auto racing—even drag racing. These photos show what happened when Frank Maratta, free-wheeling Connecticut Dragway owner, challenged him to a match race just four days before the 1968 Indy "500." Maratta's reputation for P. T. Barnumesque showbusiness and his ability to produce great drag racing action have made his somewhat remote location New England's "in" place to race and spectate. What made Mario accept? The man and the challenge.

Mario ponders: "Man! What am I doing here just four days before 'the big one'?" ▶

Prior to the races Dean Gregson, Mario and Bob Tasca (left to right)
concentrate on starting line procedures which are all-important in drag racing.

◀ Out of the chute! Andretti in the Cobra Jet Mustang (nearest the camera) won in three straight races over Maratta in the "L-88" Camaro.

Andretti seems rather amused at Maratta's apparent attitude of "Look, kid, don't worry. I'll take it easy on ya in the first round. Okay?"

It's over and they are both winners: Mario for the match race;
Frank for his promotional genius.

The Statistical Side of Mario Andretti

Mario Andretti's rise to stardom has been phenomenal. He made his Championship debut at Trenton, New Jersey in April of 1964 and in the space of six seasons, rose to second place in the USAC All-time Point Standings from 1956. In those six years he won the National Championship three times and was runnerup twice. Strangely enough, he had already become one of the best-known American drivers even before he won his first Championship event in July of 1965.

His performance in 100-mile Championship races on dirt tracks has been outstanding. He has driven twenty-seven races since 1964, finishing in the first three fifteen times and failing to score points in only five. He won five races and was second eight times. By coincidence, three of the five races he failed to score in were at DuQuoin, Illinois, where he placed fifteenth in three consecutive years.

His very first USAC appearance was at Allentown, Pennsylvania on September 21, 1963. He drove John Wergland's sprint car on a temporary permit and was fourth fastest qualifier. He has now competed in fifty-five feature events, finishing in the top twelve forty-nine times. He has won nine and has finished in the first three twenty times.

His USAC Stock debut was on August 15, 1965, at Milwaukee, Wisconsin. He blew an engine in practice and had a new one installed for qualifying. He was last to qualify, getting under way just as the deadline arrived. He set the twenty-second fastest time and it was discovered that only half the cylinders had been connected! He finished fourth.

USAC Record

Year	Division	No. of Feature Starts	Point Ranking	Wins	Seconds	Thirds	Top Three Finishes
1963	Sprints	2	—	—	—	—	—
1964	Championship	10	11th	—	—	1.	1
	Sprints	20	3rd	1	4	—	5
	Midgets	4	83rd	—	—	—	—
1965	Championship	16	1st	1	6	3	10
	Sprints	12	10th	1	1	2	4
	Midgets	1	121st	—	—	—	—
	Stocks	5	12th	—	—	1	1
1966	Championship	15	1st	8	1	—	9
	Sprints	18	2nd	5	1	3	9
	Midgets	2	64th	1	—	—	1
	Stocks	2	20th	—	—	1	1
1967	Championship	19	2nd	8	3	2	13
	Sprints	3	18th	2	—	—	2
	Midgets	1	75th	—	—	—	—
	Stocks	8	7th	1	1	—	2
1968	Championship	27*	2nd	4*	11*	1	16
	Sprints	—	—	—	—	—	—
	Midgets	—	—	—	—	—	—
	Stocks	1	20th	—	—	1	1
1969	Championship	24*	1st	9*	3*	1*	13
	Sprints	—	—	—	—	—	—
	Midgets	2	101st	—	—	—	—
	Stocks	—	—	—	—	—	—

* Includes "twin" races

Summary of Indianapolis Record

Year	Car	Speed Ranking	Qual.	Start	Finish	Laps	Speed/Reason Out	LD
1965	Dean Van Lines	4	158.849	4	3	200	149.121	200
1966	Dean Van Lines	1	165.899	1	18	27	Valve	27
1967	Dean Van Lines	1	168.982	1	30	58	Lost Wheel	58
1968	Overseas National Airways	4	167.691	4	33	2	Burned Piston	2
1968R	Overseas National Airways	(Relieved L. Dickson		15-24)	28	10	Burned Piston	10
1969	STP Oil Treatment	2	169.851	2	1	200	156.867	200
							Total laps (5 races)	497

Summary of USAC Starts and Top Three Finishes

Division	Total Starts	Wins	Seconds	Thirds	Top Three
Championship	111*	30*	24*	8	62
Sprint	55	9	6	5	20
Midget	10	1	—	—	1
Stocks	16	1	1	3	5
	192	41	31	16	88

* Includes "twin" races

Major Events Won

1964

Oct. 4	USAC	Sprint	Salem, Ind.	½P	100 laps
			Pat O'Connor-Joe James Memorial		

1965

July 25	USAC	Champ	Indpls. Raceway Park, Ind.	1⅞P-RC	150 miles
			Hoosier Grand Prix		
Nov. 6	USAC	Sprint	Gardena, Calif.	½D	30 laps

1966

June 5	USAC	Champ	Milwaukee, Wisc.	1P	100 miles
June 12	USAC	Champ	Langhorne, Pa.	1P	100 miles
June 26	USAC	Champ	Atlanta, Ga.	1½P	300 miles
July 8	USAC	Midget	Marne, Mich.	⅓P	50 laps
July 24	USAC	Champ	Indpls. Raceway Park, Ind.	1⅞P-RC	150 miles
			Hoosier Grand Prix		
July 31	USAC	Sprint	Cumberland, Md.	½D	30 laps
Aug. 27	USAC	Champ	Milwaukee, Wisc.	1P	200 miles
Aug. 28	USAC	Sprint	Oswego, N.Y.	⅝P	100 laps
Sept. 4	USAC	Sprint	Rossburg, Ohio	½D	50 laps
Sept. 10	USAC	Champ	Indpls. Fairgrounds, Ind.	1D	100 miles
			Hoosier Hundred		
Sept. 25	USAC	Champ	Trenton, N.J.	1P	200 miles
Oct. 2	USAC	Sprint	Salem, Ind.	½P	100 laps
			Pat O'Connor-Joe James Memorial		
Nov. 20	USAC	Champ	Phoenix, Ariz.	1P	200 miles
Nov. 27	USAC	Sprint	Phoenix, Ariz.	½D	30 laps

1967

Feb. 28	NASCAR	Stock	Daytona, Fla.	2½P	500 miles
			Daytona 500		
Apr. 1	FIA	Sports	Sebring, Fla.	5.2P-RC	1237.6 miles
			12 Hours of Sebring		
			Co-driving with Bruce McLaren		

Major Events Won

(Continued)

Apr. 23	USAC	Champ	Trenton, N.J.	1P	150 miles
July 16	USAC	Sprint	Oswego, N.Y.	⅝P	Twin 50 laps
			Both heats		
July 23	USAC	Champ	Indpls. Raceway Park, Ind.	1⅞P-RC	150 miles
July 29	USAC	Stock	Mosport, Canada	2½P-RC	125 miles
July 30	USAC	Champ	Langhorne, Pa.	1P	150 miles
Aug. 6	USAC	Champ	St. Jovite, Canada	2.6P-RC	200 miles
			Twin 100s (Both)		
Aug. 20	USAC	Champ	Milwaukee, Wisc.	1P	200 miles
Sept. 9	USAC	Champ	Indpls. Fairgrounds, Ind.	1D	100 miles
			Hoosier Hundred		
Nov. 19	USAC	Champ	Phoenix, Ariz.	1P	200 miles

1968

Aug. 3	USAC	Champ	St. Jovite, Canada	2.6P-RC	200 miles
			Twin 100s (Both)		
Sept. 2	USAC	Champ	DuQuoin, Ill.	1D	100 miles
Sept. 22	USAC	Champ	Trenton, N.J.	1P	200 miles

1969

Apr. 13	USAC	Champ	Hanford, Calif.	1½P	200 miles
May 30	USAC	Champ	Indianapolis, Ind.	2½P	500 miles
June 29	USAC	Champ	Pike's Peak, Colo.	Hill climb	
July 12	USAC	Champ	Nazareth, Pa.	1⅛D	100 miles
July 19	USAC	Champ	Trenton, N.J.	1½P	200 miles
Aug. 18	USAC	Champ	Springfield, Ill.	1D	100 miles
Sept. 21	USAC	Champ	Trenton, N.J.	1½P	300 miles
Oct. 19	USAC	Champ	Kent, Wash.	2.25P-RC	100 miles
			(1st heat)		
Dec. 7	USAC	Champ	Riverside, Calif.	2½P-RC	300 miles

P—Paved   D—Dirt   RC—Road Course

Mario's Five Years at Indy

1965: Started fourth (158.849 mph). Finished third. Voted Rookie of the Year. Became a member of the Champion 100-Mile-an-Hour Club.

1966: Started first (165.899 mph). Finished eighteenth. Led sixteen laps. Eliminated due to valve trouble. Became member of Autolite Pacemakers Club.

1967: Started first (168.982 mph). Finished thirtieth. Eliminated due to losing a wheel.

1968: Started fourth (167.691 mph). Finished thirty-third. Eliminated due to burned piston. Relieved Larry Dickson. Finished twenty-eighth. Eliminated due to burned piston.

1969: Started second (169.851 mph). Finished first.